The Rainbow Watchers

A Novel by
Marlene King

The Rainbow Watchers
First edition, published 2018

By Marlene King

Copyright ©2018, Marlene King

Cover Design: Tim Meikle

Cover Photo by: Pixabay

ISBN-13: 978-1-942661-92-4

This is a work of fiction. Names, characters, businesses, places, events and incidents are either the products of the author's imagination or used in a fictitious manner. Any resemblance to actual persons, living or dead, or actual events is purely coincidental.

All rights reserved. No part of this book may be reproduced or transmitted in any form or by any means, electronic or mechanical, including photocopying, recording or by any information storage and retrieval system, without written permission from the author, except for the inclusion of brief quotations in a review.

Published by Kitsap Publishing
P.O. Box 572
Poulsbo, WA 98370
www.KitsapPublishing.com

Printed in the United States of America

50-10 9 8 7 6 5 4 3 2 1

What lies beyond the veil we call death may surprise you –Elizabeth Welles, a recently widowed young woman, and a curious nun, who takes her under her spiritual wing, are about to find out. Elizabeth cannot cope with her loss and attempts to take her life only to be confronted by The Watchers who escort her on a cosmic journey that offers choice, hope and a promise of fulfillment.

What if you slept
And what if
In your sleep
You dreamed
And what if
In your dream
You went to heaven
And there plucked a strange and beautiful flower
And what if
When you awoke
You had that flower in your hand
Ah, what then?

~*Samuel Taylor Coleridge*, The Complete Poems

"To enter the realm of ***The Rainbow Watchers*** is to find yourself in a vivid, luminescent landscape of color, sparkling with gems that feel alive and were created with words! I was drawn into the unfolding story of Elizabeth's journey from loss to healing and happiness with the help of her angelic guides, family and friends. She was able to be vulnerable, but strong, as she entered into new relationships and allowed herself to embrace life again. I imagined Stephen as being in the "Rainbow" world going through his stages of healing at the same time that Elizabeth was going through hers where they each could release the past in order to embrace the future."

~ **Judith Picone**

"I started reading ***The Rainbow Watchers*** and can't put it down! I am totally immersed in its fluid, rich descriptions and characters. I was drawn in immediately, as the whole idea of ***The Rainbow Watchers*** intrigues and speaks to me. The book is well-written and is an invitation to those who may not be aware of different dimensions and the power of the colors of the chakras to explore them in a rich, varied environment. This book has "found its time," as civilization moves closer to acknowledging dimensions beyond the third and of communications beyond the thin veil that separates us from a vast, creative consciousness that can be ours if we open to it."

~ **Suzanne Parkhurst**,
Certified Qigong Instructor, Herbalist,
Reiki Practitioner and End of Life Doula

"***The Rainbow Watchers*** is an inspirational story of hope and healing. Marlene demonstrates a beautiful writing style throughout and creates peaceful guides, grief resolution and spiritual intervention that lead to a "feel good" outcome. I appreciated the emphasis on deep friendships and homespun values woven into each chapter and fully appreciate her rich use of colorful vocabulary and the unfolding of a touching story."

~ **Candis Fancher,**
Speech Therapist, Certified Grief Facilitator

"By creating an unforgettable, mystical, heavenly realm and folding it seamlessly into a richly imagined story of redemption, *The Rainbow Watchers* gives us two most precious gifts --- the uplifting feelings of both hope and love."

~ **Leslie L. Hamel**, Kingston, WA

"The engaging reality in *The Rainbow Watchers* is an uplifting journey of expansion and hope. Marlene King's vision, verity, and spirit shine."

~ **Marci Madsen Fuller,** Author, *Crosscurrents*

"In *The Rainbow Watchers*, Elizabeth's enigmatic NDE beautifully illustrates the connection between our human chakras to the color bands in the rainbow. It opens the pathway to the power of love and ability to trust that the integration of our spiritual nature is always at work in our lives."

~ **Sandra Custer**, MSW

"Marlene helps you see in *The Rainbow Watchers* the importance of paying attention to our rich inner dream life and what is waiting to be awakened. The heartfelt resonance of being in relationship with the Divine drives this story which I found both reassuring and illuminating. It's not every day that spiritual ideas and beings are so lovingly woven within a literary landscape."

~ **Ann Wilkinson Ellis,** Producer of *Still with Thee* (Inspirational Recording), Co-producer of *Farewell to Harry*, (Independent Film), Teacher, Director, Actor, Writer

"The *Rainbow Watchers* is a touching tale about the transfiguration of loss. It takes readers out over the perilous edge then sets us free to remember we are here to risk ourselves to each other, and the world, while discovering who we are being called to be, and become."

~ **Sandra Wallin, B.Sc., B.Ed., M.A.**
Belief Builder & Change Agent,
Founder of Chiron's Way Center for Equine Guided Development

Dedication

To all who have ever experienced darkness or despair, there is always a choice to move out of the shadows and into the light. To The Watchers whose eternal presence guides us from the rainbows whether we believe it or not.

Chapter One

The Beginning of the End

A UPS truck barreled past the window and broke her concentration. Annoyed, she scowled, hit "save" on the keyboard and stood up to see a brown truck zip in a driveway a few houses down the street. He was driving too fast for this vintage neighborhood, and she vowed to suggest installing speed bumps at the next block meeting. Before she eased back into her ergonomic chair, she noted that the blossoms were beginning to split open on the branches of the cherry trees that lined the street. She returned her attention to the graphic design she was working on that consisted of foliage and shadows against a cluster of high-rise buildings.

Minutes later, her cell phone buzzed underneath a pile of documents that littered her workstation. She shoved the papers aside and saw the phone screen indicated the call was from St. John's Hospital. She wondered what they wanted and despite the fact it might be a solicitation, she answered just in case, since her husband was out on his run early this morning.

"May I speak with Mrs. Elizabeth Welles? Her name was listed as the emergency contact for Stephen Welles."

The over-sized monitor with its panoramic spread of buildings kaleidoscoped in front of her. "This is Elizabeth Welles. Has something happened to my husband?" Elizabeth shot up from her chair, paced nervously and bit her lip. Time collapsed like ruins around her and the room was spinning.

The man's voice was low, even and kind. "I'm Dr. Wallace Meade in the ER at St. John's Hospital and I'm very sorry to inform you that your husband, Stephen, was found in distress along the Maple Heights Trail this morning. The jogger who discovered him called emergency services and Mr. Welles was transported to our facility where we were unable to revive him."

Elizabeth froze, incapable to absorb the information, trust her hearing or find words. She imagined the air had been sucked from her lungs and she held her head to stop the ringing.

"Mrs. Welles? Are you still there? We'll need you to come down and make arrangements. Is there anyone who can drive you? May we call someone? I realize this is a tremendous shock."

Elizabeth regained her breath, snapped out of her trance and shouted into the phone, "Nooooo, it's not true! Nooo, not Stephen! You must be wrong. He's due back any minute—he just left a little bit ago. We had coffee before he went out for his jog and . . ." Visceral emotion washed over her vibrating body. Sobs and a violent storm of tears flowed as she collapsed onto her office couch screaming in someone else's voice.

❧ ❧ ❧

Elizabeth let her closest friend from work, Marni Petrakis, guide and support her through the hospital entrance to the reception desk where she saw a nun chatting with the desk attendant.

The nun looked up and saw the hunched over body of a young woman who was clearly suffering with the weight of crisis.

Elizabeth registered comprehension in the nun's expression and knew she had witnessed grief many times. Marni explained to the receptionist why they were there and the two women were directed to a waiting area off the main corridor.

Elizabeth and Marni were alone in the intimate blue-green carpeted room. The interior colors were cool and subdued with several chairs upholstered in a mid-century modern design grouped around contemporary walnut end tables.

Marni fidgeted and comforted her friend with kind words and a supply of tissues, but Elizabeth stared ahead, numb and detached.

Elizabeth tumbled through a surreal portal and retreated to a space without time, reeling from the insanity of being in a hospital setting and the words she replayed telling her that Stephen was dead.

There was a soft knock on the door before a distinguished gray-haired man of about fifty in a hospital lab coat opened it and entered holding a tablet in the crook of his arm.

Marni stood and introduced herself to him. "I'm Marni Petrakis, Mrs. Welles' friend. This is such a shock."

He nodded and turned his attention to Elizabeth. "Mrs. Welles? I'm Dr. Meade and I was with your husband when he died. I'm sorry, we did everything we could. Were you aware of an existing heart condition?"

Elizabeth shook her head, dazed, face swollen.

"Would you like to be with him?" the doctor offered. His compassion was well-practiced, but genuine.

"Do what feels right, Liz. Don't have any regrets."

Elizabeth's voice was almost inaudible. "Will you come with me?"

The doctor escorted both women down a brightly lit hallway to an anteroom where Stephen lay.

❧ ❧ ❧

Elizabeth rarely left her house. It had been a couple of months since Stephen's memorial service in April. She barely got through the experience, much less remembered it, as her grief was all-consuming which made her go deeper into a dark place. She did not bathe regularly or get dressed for the day, return calls, eat properly or pick up her mail. Her world slid into an abyss after Stephen's untimely death.

A photo taken last September by the server in their favorite restaurant was one of her treasured mementos. They were celebrating their fourth anniversary. Displayed in a showy frame on a living room side table, she picked it up on her way to the kitchen. She thought a cup of tea might revive her spirits, so she filled a kettle and opened the tea canister and located a clean mug. She sat at the breakfast bar and studied the photo while she waited for the water to boil. She searched for a clue on their faces which were frozen in time that would indicate that six months later her beloved Stephen would be dead at thirty-eight. This was a man who ran several miles a day and did all the right things to maintain his health, but was taken by a rare congenital heart defect that was never detected or diagnosed. Their future plans were severed at the hands of an evil fate or whatever decides these mortal punishments in the pitiful lives of humankind. Elizabeth was bitter and went in circles with rage and sadness, the depths of which she had never before experienced.

The doorbell rang just as the kettle started to whistle. Elizabeth, jolted from her reverie, got up and turned off the gas and padded to the entry. She checked the peephole and opened the door to her neighbor who stood there with a thermal slow cooker in her hands.

"Mrs. Goldstein."

"I made extra and thought you might appreciate soup for supper," she held out the pot to Elizabeth with a bright, genuine smile.

"Thank you. I was just making tea. Would you . . . ?" Before Elizabeth could finish her sentence, Mrs. Goldstein was inside the foyer and looking around.

"That would be lovely, dear," and made her way to the kitchen and set the pot on the counter next to the stove. Elizabeth trotted behind. "How are you doing? Manny and I have been very worried about you. The blinds are never up and we hardly ever see you leave." A slight flush traveled across her cheeks betraying her proclivity to keep her eye on her neighbors' business. She opened the top button of her cardigan.

"I have good days and bad days, but guess that's normal, or at least that's what they tell me." Elizabeth got the water up to a boil again and pulled another mug from the shelf. "Lipton?" she asked, knowing it was the only tea she ever saw her neighbor drink and Elizabeth had a habit of always keeping a supply of it in her pantry.

"Of course." Mrs. Goldstein studied her neighbor carefully. "Who tells you it's normal?"

Elizabeth placed the teabags into the cups and poured scalding water over them. It reminded her of the grief that scalded her inside. "Oh, I went to a few support groups after, uh, Stephen passed. I didn't get a lot out of them—it seemed futile. Not a lot one can say about grief except that it's hell." She pushed the mug and a sugar bowl toward her neighbor.

"If there is ever anything we can do, we are just next door and I'm only working part time now, but soon I'll be home permanently."

"Oh, I didn't know. You're finally going to retire! Good for you."

"October. Manny's been wanting me to quit for years so I can be home with him. He doesn't miss a day of corporate life. We have an extended trip planned for several weeks after I get my golden parachute."

Mrs. Goldstein doctored her tea with a generous amount of sugar. "Our daughter Nadine and her husband, Myron, will be staying in our house while we're away and wanted you to know. I'm sure they would be happy to look in on you or . . ."

"I'll be fine, Mrs. Goldstein, but thanks for the heads up. Elizabeth swirled the tea in her cup and glanced at the photo she left on the counter. "Without family, it's a challenge sometimes. My brother's in California and we're not close. He only met Stephen once at our wedding and it'd been years since there'd been any contact." Elizabeth toyed with the soggy string and tag dangling over her cup. "I appreciate all you've already done."

Mrs. Goldstein smiled and poked a strand of hair behind her ear enjoying the acknowledgment and nodded toward the pot on the counter. "I brought you my special-recipe potato soup. It's hearty and looks like you could use it. Your arms need some meat on them." Mrs. Goldstein was outspoken, but truthful. "Did Stephen have family?" she asked from left field.

"Just an older sister who lives in Europe. I've never met her. She's a scientist of some prominence and travels the world, but was always too busy to schedule a visit. She didn't even make it to his memorial service, but sent a lovely spray of flowers with her condolences." Elizabeth uttered with a slight constriction in her throat.

"I see. Families can be strange no matter what. But they are the ties that bind. Perhaps you could reach out and invite her here or you could visit her? Have you thought about traveling? I have this amazing travel agent."

Elizabeth stood and put her cup in the sink, her way of announcing the conversation was growing tedious. She was exhausted and although her neighbor was well-intentioned, she needed space. Her nerves were shredded and she felt edgy and anxious most of the time, as if there was something else she was supposed to be doing, but she didn't know what. Elizabeth expressed her gratitude for the soup and escorted Mrs. Goldstein to the front door.

🙢 🙢 🙢

It was nearing the summer solstice and the nights were warm. Elizabeth slept with her window ajar, as the night air energized her especially when it was charged with ions from summer storms. She lay awake for several hours peering outside and thought about her recurring dream and wondered if she would have it tonight. It always left her with unsettled feelings and imagery that tapped into another time and place. She first had the dream shortly after Stephen died. It was usually the same scenario with minor variations. She found herself in a chamber with ancient Doric columns with lush flowers and shrubbery crowding the perimeters. There were shadowy beings milling around performing rituals. They held earthen bowls of smoldering incense and fanned a circle of smoke around her body with a large feather as they chanted in a chorus of foreign words and bowed rhythmically. No one looked at her directly, but their otherworldly appearance and manner was intense and their billowy garments reminded her of magician's capes. She then laid down on the skin of a leopard, closed her eyes and surrendered to a strange euphoria. Before long, she could feel and smell musky-scented oils applied to her forehead and feet. With that, she bolted awake to find herself on her back absorbed in the familiar feeling that lingered from an ancient time.

Chapter Two

Down the Rabbit Hole

The humidity and triple digit temperatures were unbearable that August. Elizabeth lowered the temperature in her pearl-white Prius and cranked up the fan and radio and tilted the interior vents toward her face. Her fine light brown hair was tied with an elastic band to keep it off her neck, but the skin on the back of her legs stuck to the seat. She loved the ocean and had not been since she and Stephen spent a few vacation days there last summer. Today she wanted to empty her lingering grief and painful emotions into the sea to be swallowed up and carried away with the tide.

The over-the-top amount of traffic matched the temperatures with people escaping the city heat. Elizabeth chose a shortcut off the main highway and wound through coastal towns, most of which were disheveled remnants of early Americana. But the modern age was everywhere and the Walgreens on the corner of Morgan Street and First Avenue was the landmark to turn right which would take her directly to a public beach access location. Usually there were just a handful of beach-goers, but today dozens of cars clogged the small parking area. Lowering her window, she breathed in the briny breeze, cool and inviting. She squeezed into a spot between a tuft of tall sea grass and a metallic-blue SUV. A white wave of heat shimmered along the shoreline where people splashed in the surf.

Leaving the windows cracked, she pulled out a sand chair, wide-brimmed floppy hat and a thermal bag packed with snacks and water and reading material from the back seat. She kept her flip-flops on as the sand was blistering. Maneuvering down a sandy path, she found a semi-quiet spot apart from the crowds next to a sand bank that was set back several yards from the water.

When she spread her towel, she remembered the times she and Stephen made this trip. A rush of emptiness and fear permeated her body, but she attempted to keep her attention on the ritual of setting up her space, even though a few tears escaped from the corners of her eyes. She positioned the chair and liberally sprayed SPF on her arms, legs and torso and watched children laugh and splash in the waves and couples stop to pick up shells and meander along the edge of the water. They reminded her of the possibilities of what might have been with Stephen that were cut short. Recognizing she was about to slip again into that painful space that caused her throat and solar plexus to contract, she challenged herself to shift her focus. Settling into the chair on her towel, she cleaned her sunglasses, pulled the brim on her hat down to block the sun and opened up her book. Attempting to stay conscious, she read the words, stayed with the words, but her mind inevitably wandered and found grief in the shadows. It had to get better, and some days it was, but not today. She turned to the pounding waves that set a rhythm and lured her back to be in the moment, and for that, she was grateful.

When the sun moved lower on the horizon, Elizabeth checked the time and messages on her cell. There was a text from Marni and two voicemails from her boss. She did not know how she deserved their loyalty, as her moods and energy were often dark and tentative. Fred, her boss, had questions about a past project and Marni wanted to catch a movie—hang out in an air-conditioned theatre. That part sounded good, since the mantle of heat in the east squeezed out the last vestiges of summer with a vengeance. After Labor Day, the days shortened and the grip of summer relaxed and the magic of fall entered through the back door. She punched in a reply, gathered her belongings and made her way to the car hoping to beat the lion's share of traffic back into the city.

The smell of popcorn in theatre lobbies evoked memories. Whenever she and Stephen went to the movies, they shared the big tub with extra butter. The iconic treat created an expectation of escape, being transported into the fantasyland of film.

Marni wore a sleeveless, powder-blue checkered sundress and Elizabeth, a gauzy peasant top over cropped pants. They looked younger than their years and despite the sunscreen, Elizabeth's skin glowed pink and obliterated the pasty pallor she was accustomed to the last few months.

"Extra butter, please," Marni added to her order. The young teen boy blushed when she looked directly at him with her dark and enormous Mediterranean eyes. "Want the same, Liz? You could use it."

It had been a while since Elizabeth's appetite was piqued. "Okay. I'll have extra butter." Marni had a way of taking her up to the top floor whether she wanted to go or not.

☙ ☙ ☙

Elizabeth begged off going to a club after the movie. Marni insisted it would do her good, but Liz convinced her otherwise. She was not ready to be in that type of environment and the thought of it made her stomach churn. Her energy spent, she said good night to her friend in the theatre parking lot. It was balmy out and she drove home with the windows down and contemplated Marni's suggestion. Going out again, the dating scene. It was the last thing on her mind, and wondered if she would ever feel like it. A flood of tears surprised her and she felt lonelier than she ever had before.

She parked in the garage and after lowering the door, realized she forgot to leave the porch light on. Standing by the side of the house in the dark, she tried several keys until the door to the mudroom opened. She entered and bolted the door behind her.

The house was stuffy. She opened a few windows to let the hot air escape and set the air at sixty-eight degrees to cool it off. She remembered Stephen always took care of these things. Missing him crushed her. She was thirsty from the popcorn and felt like she had swallowed a bucket of dust so grabbed a bottle of chilled water in the fridge. She unscrewed the cap and took a long drink on her way to her bedroom. Elizabeth decided she would never sleep without her meds tonight and extracted a vial of "magic pills" from her nightstand drawer, opened it and shook one into her palm. Her docs would only write scripts for ten at a time now because her depression lingered and she did not show signs of being able to accept her circumstances. There was liability if she harmed herself or others. And since she did not consent to go to a shrink or groups or anything else suggested to assist her grieving, they limited her access to potentially deadly medications. So she took them sparingly. She popped one into her mouth and the icy water felt good going down. She wondered what it would be like if she took all of them that she managed to hoard from when they gave them to her plentifully around the time of the Stephen's death. But tonight, getting some sleep was all she wanted.

She closed the windows, adjusted the thermostat to seventy-five degrees and took a cool shower to lower her core temperature. The humidity was oppressive. As she stood under the mist of the rain shower head, she dared to think about taking her brother up on his offer to go to California. There was nothing there to remind her of Stephen, but plenty to remind her of the parts of her life she would rather not remember. Conservative and shy by nature, fitting in with trendy groups, clubs or cliques was impossible. She was lost in a sea of people and the pain from the loss of both parents early in life was overwhelming to experience essentially alone. And, there was only one season of the year versus four and the pace was staggering. She had made a life in New England during the past decade and it felt like home. It was home. Marni suggested she sell her house and move into a condo. There would be little or no maintenance and she could make it her own. Besides, she might meet someone. Marni rightly pointed out that she and Stephen bought into an "established" neighborhood with few people their own age. The thought of being able to come and go in new surroundings was appealing and had merit, but it was too soon to make that decision—either way. The more she thought about the unknowns of her future, the more she turned to the comfort and security of the past and she realized she would have to leave one of them behind.

૪ ૪ ૪

That night she dreamed of the chamber and shot straight up in bed fully awake when she thought she smelled the incense and aromatic oils. The green digital numerals on her clock displayed 3:34 a.m. when she got up and looked outside. No cars going by at this time of the morning. She finished the bottle of water on the nightstand, used the bathroom and went back to bed hoping the sleeping pill would carry her back to the Land of Nod on the coattails of morning.

Chapter Three

The Homecoming

The off-white walls glowed gray under the fluorescent lights of the hospital room. Elizabeth squinted at the ceiling tiles dotted with sprinkler heads and wrinkled her nose at the antiseptic bite in the air. An unearthly fog drifted in and out of her head blurring her focus, but through partially open blinds, she managed to glimpse the last gasp of the day held hostage in the hands of magnificent scarlet skies. She faded in and out of consciousness, remembering the rain, heavy and insistent. The dullness of her drug-affected state was like concrete in her veins pinning her to the institutional sheets that chafed her bony elbows. Elizabeth Welles had been to the end of the line and back. The bedside monitor beat out rhythms that measured her life, and thin plastic tubes pumped clear liquids into her fragile arms.

As comprehension of the failure to end her life set in, fear swept through Elizabeth's slender chest and released a flood into her ash-colored eyes. She had no choice but to surrender to humiliation and recede into a black pool of unconsciousness where she succumbed and fell into a fitful sleep.

The rustle of Sister Antoinette's crepe skirts and light footsteps added to the hospital room's clinical undercurrent. The good Sister checked on Elizabeth whose stone-still body was draped with a pastel pink coverlet. She had ministered to the frail woman from the time of her admission two days ago, looking in at regular intervals, hoping to catch her awake.

Antoinette considered Elizabeth's intake history, and it was evident she was overwhelmed by the storms of life. The Sister held a clear memory of the crumpled woman who had come to identify and retrieve her husband's body seven months ago. It was not her place, clinically, to investigate further, but spiritually was another matter. Antoinette deemed Elizabeth had not finished her assignment in this world, and resolved to fan any hope the young woman may have into flames of salvation and redemption.

Antoinette's mission stirred into a fierce vigilance to ensure Elizabeth's destiny would be played out and her soul saved. When the nun dragged an orange plastic chair across the floor to the edge of the bed, wobbly metal discs screeched. Closing her eyes, Sister Antoinette prayed, holding her jet-beaded rosary, as if it were alive.

Elizabeth did not react to the swish of crepe when the Sister left her bedside.

Only the light from the monitors and ambient glow from the hall were visible when Elizabeth made an attempt to fully open her eyes for the first time in days. Numbness embroidered the periphery of her consciousness, as she cautiously struggled to grasp the scope of her surroundings. Elizabeth labored to figure out the smudge of faces and conversations that slid into mental quicksand. She moaned in frustration and her sense of loss was visceral masked by the residue of narcotics that came close to claiming her life.

The effort to push herself into a sitting position made Elizabeth's head pound. Months of lessened activity had weakened her muscles, and she slumped onto her back observing the needles and connections to tubes and bags. The exertion propelled her to the threshold of dreams, patterns of shards, captives in the prison of her mind. Before she allowed them to overtake her, she lay in a twilight reverie.

The door to her small private room was half open opposite her bed. She observed a crew mopping the corridor floors, their shadows diffused in low light. The night sounds of other patients, muffled voices, shuffling noises drifted in. Nurses performed midnight rounds, wafting down the hall on rubber-soled shoes that stilled the echoes of their presence.

Elizabeth's breathing reminded her that she had survived the attempt to end her life and she resented it. The effort she took to ensure this would not happen was futile. Her meticulous plan to ingest the stash of pills she amassed after Stephen's death would have allowed her to join him. She spent considerable hours researching how much dosage would be lethal and she coyly courted the pharmacist to validate her calculations. Now she was confused and sad and would have to live with the embarrassment and pain.

Her eyes grew accustomed to the dim pallor of the room and maybe an hour passed, or two, there was no way to measure for sure before she saw a large black dog wandering down the hallway, its nose to the floor sniffing until it found her door. Startled, Elizabeth watched it pause and cross the threshold into her room with a playful bound. Ignoring her light whistle, it circled checking out every corner. It stopped, stood rigid, perked its ears and returned to the hallway, evaporating before it reached the door. Convincing herself she was either dreaming or hallucinating, Elizabeth believed her stupor created the experience. She wanted to sleep and move away from the encroaching memories of Stephen and her failure, but faces crowded in. She could see dear Marni, shaking her and crying and the Goldsteins paralyzed with fear. She observed emergency room attendants shove tubes down her throat and pierce her flesh with needles. Surrounded by demons of torment, something distracted her. Through a tear in the veil she saw a flicker of another dimension. It was a garden, glowing with wild beds of brilliant red flowers shrouded by a crimson sky and a mist that drew her in.

It was easy to follow the path that edged the garden. The clouds levitated over the landscape and the fragrance from the blooms aroused Elizabeth. It was like a rich rosebud wine, a heady mixture of red velvet and Victorian perfume. A small course of stepping-stones, heart-shaped aggregates, like the ones in her parents' garden invited her to go deeper into the floral shrubbery. Looking up, the childhood saying of "red skies at night . . . a sailor's delight" came to mind. It portended the dawn of a glorious day. Luxuriating in the thought, she mingled among thousands of scarlet flowers that flourished in every direction.

❧ ❧ ❧

After matins in the convent chapel, Sister Antoinette reflected on her prayers during her daily walk to St. John's, one of New England's oldest and finest healing institutions. The late September air was sharp, the sky cloudless and pristine from the downpour the day before. Reaching the marble entrance of the foyer, her mind turned to her official duties as a clinical spiritual counselor. She had served apprenticeships and received her formal education under these auspices, feeling blessed to have been assigned this post. Her tenure of more than thirty years was legendary; an esteemed fixture of the Order.

The briefings with hospital staff were routine. She checked her roster of patients, the evening chartings, then took the elevator to Elizabeth's ward on the fourth floor. A thermal food cart was in the hall where an orderly slid out a breakfast tray with Elizabeth's name and room number on it. Antoinette waited outside while he placed it on the rolling table next to the bedside. He filled a fresh pitcher of ice with water at the sink then poured a glass half-full and stripped the wrapping off a straw and popped it into the glass. Antoinette stared hard at Elizabeth through rimless spectacles. Both compassion and fear for her young soul clutched the nun's buxom chest. Hot tea and a covered bowl of cream of rice cooled, as Elizabeth began to rouse with the orderly's cheerful banter. The Sister knew the aides would arrive soon to perform their hygiene regimen, but she wanted to be present when Elizabeth was fully awake. And she was not disappointed.

Chapter Four

The Invitation

On Elizabeth's third day of hospitalization, her eyes winced at the glare as she accustomed herself to the light. A young nurse's aide bobbed underneath the fluorescent lights and her tight curls shone like copper wire wrapped around spools. She stripped the stale gown from Elizabeth, then pulled her thin arms through the sleeves of a fresh faded print hospital garment. Turning her onto her side, the aide slathered a medicinal-smelling lotion across Elizabeth's spine and shoulders, then tied the garment at the neck and rolled her over. She vigorously massaged the lotion onto Elizabeth's arms and elbows, its clean aroma grew stronger. Elizabeth vaguely recalled a scrap of a dream where she was massaged with oils and felt nurtured in the young girl's skilled hands. The aide squeezed a washcloth from the basin of hot water on the tray table and wiped strands of hair off Elizabeth's face. The warmth of the washcloth soothed her delicate skin and revived her. Imagining she had been in bed for a century, Elizabeth moaned as she moved her limbs, the IV and catheter tubes straining against her. She was reminded of the grief and shame streaming throughout her body, and closed her eyes to shut out the world.

After the white-jacketed aide left the room, she felt a hand lightly touch the top of her head. She peered through small slits between her lids and saw the lined face of an elderly woman in a navy-blue skirt and jacket with a white turtleneck jersey underneath.

"I'm Sister Antoinette. Would you like some tea?"

Elizabeth shook her head.

"Or a sip of water, perhaps?"

"Uhmmm, yes," the nun held the glass to Elizabeth's lips that found the flexible straw and she drank.

"I've been praying for your recovery." The Sister's polite tone and demeanor appeared to Elizabeth as a mask of normalcy to stabilize her.

"You're in St. John's," the Sister said, with a morsel of reverence. "You were transported here from New Bristol's emergency clinic three days ago."

"I'm not Catholic," Elizabeth disclosed.

"You're a soul in pain and I've been concerned about your welfare since I first saw you several months ago." Antoinette looked pointedly into Elizabeth's pale gray eyes and she said, "I'm a good listener."

Elizabeth's mind flashed on the pills, how hard it was and how long it took to swallow the dozens she had squirreled away. She had not bargained for how long it would take—it gave her time to think, reconsider, but she pushed through with steel resolve. Then there were the jumbled days with little sleep or food in the shadow of depression after Stephen's death and the visions and dreams tucked somewhere in between.

Sister Antoinette was in a chair by the bed, perched like bird.

"My husband died several months ago . . . you must know. I think I may have seen you here the day he died. I feel ashamed." Elizabeth's eyes welled and the thin cotton pillowcase absorbed her tears. Turning her head away from the Sister, she felt Antoinette's hand gently pressing on hers.

"There is no need for shame. Are you a person of faith?"

Elizabeth smothered her sobs. "I don't know. I'm not sure of anything—what's real and what isn't. I've started remembering visions and dreams, people crowding in on me. And I saw a dog run through the hallway and into this room, but it left after snooping around. Do they allow dogs in here?"

Antoinette's eyes widened and her breathing sped up at the mention of the black dog. "There have been patient reports about a black dog roaming the halls. Maybe it's a pet visit to comfort a patient." Antoinette withheld the part about if the dog did not stay in their rooms, the patient survived death.

"It's confusing. I don't think you can help me, but there was this dream or a memory of a beautiful place that was very peaceful." Elizabeth turned on her side, pulling the IV line tight across her body.

Antoinette sat up straighter then leaned in closer when Elizabeth mentioned she recalled a memory or vision, using it as a segue. "I talked with your friend who was here when they brought you in and learned we have something in common, Elizabeth. I lost my mother at an early age, too," Antoinette said, letting the silence fall into the shape of a hook.

The fine furrows between Elizabeth's brows deepened, contemplating the statement. It catapulted her into the past, and the door holding her memories hostage cracked open.

"I never knew my mother, so I have nothing to miss," Elizabeth said, matter-of-fact. "My brother and dad suffered more than I. When did your mother die?"

Sister Antoinette responded, "There were pictures, of course, but I was about two and have no real memory of her. I later learned that those who grow up without mothers have a unique experience of this world." Antoinette looked pointedly at her patient. "Your mother died in childbirth?"

"She was only forty-one, but probably too old to be having babies," Elizabeth replied with resentment in her tone and stared at a corner of the room.

Antoinette chose her next words carefully. "Your accent tells me you are not from the New England area originally?"

"I grew up in L.A., but went to college here on the East Coast. I'd always been drawn to New England—seemed old world, traditional, settled, and it felt like a natural time to make the change." Elizabeth twisted the sheet into a small cone shape. "I believe it was because I was supposed to meet Stephen. He was waiting for me. We met in art school in New York." Tears blurred her vision and she looked away from the nun's gaze. "Oh, God, it's hard. I can't believe he's been gone over six months."

"What happened, dear?" Antoinette prodded with soft compassion in her voice.

Barely audible, Elizabeth whispered, "His heart, something weird, no one knew—it had gone undetected until . . ."

"Your brother was here several times, but you were not awake. I believe he had to return home due to his job and family. I know he's very worried about you, Elizabeth."

"He must be embarrassed. I don't know what to say to him." The tears ended and anger moved in. "God, I hate this. Why couldn't it be over?"

"It was God's will, my dear Elizabeth. Your life has meaning. You don't see that now, but you will," Antoinette stated with conviction.

"I don't want a life without Stephen. He was my world. We'd been talking about children—making plans for our future," Elizabeth rubbed her puffy eyes.

"There's always hope and the promise of tomorrow. I know you will realize this one day." Antoinette's platitudes were rote and inadequate, so she plied a refocusing technique. "Tell me about your work."

"I let my main contracts go after Stephen died. I took on a few small projects, but lost interest." Elizabeth sighed looking into the nun's eyes that reflected the cultivated charity in her soul. "I'm a graphic illustrator. I do digital renderings of commercial architectural projects mainly. I've also done fine art—historical subjects. I've always loved New England architecture."

"I see. You must be quite talented. Talents are God's gifts to share," Antoinette's mouth pursed shut.

Elizabeth was not ready to hear that she mattered to the world.

"You must rest. Is there anything I can do for you?"

Elizabeth shook her head and closed her eyes pulling up the covers to her chin.

Sister Antoinette rose from her chair. "I'll look in on you later." She retreated with her signature rustle of skirts and her practiced clinical step.

Elizabeth, left to contemplate the Sister's conversation, drew in the memory of the red garden and drifted into a quiet abyss of sleep.

❧ ❧ ❧

The three-thirty afternoon shift rotated, and a new charge nurse checked Elizabeth's chart. She roused Elizabeth and took her vital signs. "It's time to get you up, young lady," a nasally voice announced. "Let's remove that catheter and get you into the bathroom. The walk will do your muscles good."

Elizabeth read the name Sally Devers on her badge.

"I'll send someone in to help you shortly," Sally said, leaving the room in her white-coated efficiency.

Sitting up was an effort for Elizabeth, but manageable. She stretched and rubbed her eyes awake.

An LPN appeared, a large Black woman who was about to ply her remarkable skills. "I'm your Florence Nightingale," her grin revealed a space between her two front teeth. She pointed at her name badge. Florence Trotter was etched in white against a blue background. "From the minute my mama named me, she knew I'd be a nurse."

A faint smile formed on Elizabeth's chapped lips.

Florence tossed back the covers, lifted Elizabeth's gown and removed the catheter in an instant. She swabbed the exit area with a sterile cloth, checked the IV and entered a notation on the chart. Swinging Elizabeth's legs over the side of the bed, she positioned the pole with the saline drip bag to the side and slid Elizabeth's feet into the over-sized hospital-issue white terry mules.

Grateful for Florence's hefty size, Elizabeth leaned against the nurse and drew herself up. Her knees nearly buckled, but after a few labored steps, she made it to the bathroom. With Florence's aid, she sat down on the cold split seat on the toilet. Her head was light, but nurse Sally was right—it did her good to move her muscles. She felt like she had to urinate, but the catheter had created a false pressure. After a few minutes, she called to Florence to help her up, and they made the journey back to bed where she returned to straightened sheets. Lying back onto pillows that supported her shoulders and neck, she thanked the kind nurse and felt the cold call button in her hand.

"If you need anything, just press this. Don't get up without assistance. You did real well, now, and it will make you stronger."

Florence's ample brown arms shoved the rolling table over Elizabeth's lap. She checked the water and brought her a new ice-filled carafe. After pulling the white drape halfway around the bed, Florence left humming, "Amazing Grace."

Elizabeth's head started to clear and the events that led to her suicide attempt invaded her thoughts. She allowed herself to recount her decision that evening to take the overdose to end her suffering. Her heart ached for Stephen. How could she explain to her brother, Doug, and dear Marni, who saved her life, about the depth of her pain. When Stephen died, part of her did, too. Nothing in her thirty-four years of living had prepared her for the unfathomable. No healthy male, an avid jogger, who tried for a healthy diet most of the time and was a low-stress lifestyle person dies of heart failure at thirty-eight. She could not stop the shock waves or accept the loss. Until now. Her relationship with death had changed, and she saw it from the point of her own survival.

Hearing voices in the hall, Elizabeth could see visitors arriving with flowers and smiles for their loved ones. Sitting up more easily now, she reached for the water glass and glimpsed the sweep of Sister Antoinette entering the room. She was carrying a large bouquet of deep red roses. The white porcelain vase contrasted beautifully and the velvet burgundy bow accented the flowers' rich color.

"These are for you. A card is attached," Antoinette beamed. She held them close to Elizabeth so she could breathe in their scent and pulled the card from its plastic holder.

Elizabeth was touched. She read the card, "We love you. The kids send special hugs. See you soon, Doug and Jenna."

"Thank you," Elizabeth said, grateful. She and Doug were separated by their years and distance between coastlines, but he was all she had. "They're from my brother and his family." Staring into the beauty of the roses, Elizabeth saw a luscious red invitation, a pathway to memory and the sweet essence of angels engulfed the air.

Sister Antoinette sat beside her near the bed, but Elizabeth's eyes remained on the flowers and a faint smile brushed across her lips. Transfixed, Elizabeth remembered. "Sister, I want to tell you about what I experienced when I died." Her voice sounded steady and clear, as her eyes fell shut. Her sudden peaceful state was a notable departure from her behavior just a few hours earlier.

Antoinette crossed herself and held her crucifix until it burned in her palm.

Chapter Five

Red

Elizabeth's voice was clear, but slightly monotone, when she recounted what she saw in her mind. "There was a mist that drew me into a garden where acres of plants were in bloom. I moved along a path among the terraced beds, yet I had no sensation of walking. There were roses, geraniums, daisies and asters in varying shades of red. When I inhaled their scent, I was certain they germinated from somewhere near the heart of the God. I stopped and let my senses absorb the beauty around me." Within her trance-like state, Elizabeth sighed, her mind retracing details. A flush rose on her face, as she described her experience.

Antoinette checked around the half-drawn bed curtain to see if any hospital personnel hovered. To ensure they would not be interrupted, she tiptoed the short distance to the door, closed it without a sound and returned to Elizabeth's bedside, her flesh molding into the hard organic shape of the institutional chair.

Elizabeth's calm demeanor and fixed concentration sprang from a place where ecstasy and mystery blended. She spoke with a voice embroidered in reverie. "A few wisps of vapor skirted a trellis next to an arbor laced with miniature climbing roses. The atmosphere looked airbrushed, tinged with rose, reflecting the red in the landscape. When I approached the covered walkway, the vapor transformed into two beings who extended their hands. The dark one spoke.

"'You have found your way, Elizabeth.'

"I felt no fear. Instead, bliss consumed me, and I nodded. Their presence was comforting. They turned and swept underneath the archway to the end of the arbor. I trailed behind, almost able to touch the tips of their garments, full sheets of gossamer silk, wafting in front of me. A heavy scent of roses flowed like an elixir in their wake. I felt a lightness in my body, and I adjusted to their pace, gliding in unison.

"We came to a place where a dazzling white gazebo rose out of a field of red clover, far beyond the portal at the end of the arbor. It was girdled by rows of rhododendrons three deep and their ruby-colored blooms glowed like bright jewels in the sunlight. Magically, I moved across the meadow and up the gazebo's steps and onto the platform with my companions. I followed their lead and sat on a gleaming white bench that ran along the inside of low wainscoted walls. A loving radiance emanated from the two beings. Grateful, I drank in the peace, before they spoke again.

"'You have come to the land of the red vibration,' the silken-haired one said. His voice was musical. His eyes were magnetic whirlpools of blue light.

"'You gave us permission, Elizabeth, to prepare you for a journey through the rings of life that encircle the Earth and reverberate into infinity. You have come to regain the knowledge seeded in your soul when it entered the third dimension. Your task is completion, but you were confused and have not finished your commitments there.' His luminous eyes communicated that he knew everything about me. Uncomfortable, I shifted my attention to the other being. His deep claret-colored gown, edged with fine gold thread, draped loosely across wide shoulders, gave off a dusky rose petal scent. He did not speak, but held a discerning look. I sensed his ancientness, and it humbled me.

"'You agreed to this meeting before you were born. But, you have opened the door prematurely, so you may now explore these dimensions. Each one has its own color frequency where choirs of angelic beings sing their harmonies throughout the universe. We chose not to participate with the others who fell victim to the tantalizing desires of humans and were rewarded by being allowed to dwell here.' His dark companion nodded agreement. His eyes held me transfixed as he continued, 'This is the entrance to the red realm, closest to the Earth, where life's passions connect through vibrational patterns.'

"His light hair and skin against the ripe crimson of his garment was breathtaking and disarming, but I found my voice. Currents of unconditional love and protectiveness seduced me into an unexpected sense of complicity with these ethereal beings. I directed a question to both of them. Looking around, I asked, 'Everything here is familiar. Have I been here with you before?'

"The dark one spoke, 'We existed before time—we are the oldest creation. We have always lived and are the way-showers to regions you sought when you tried to escape the Earth by your own hand.' His black eyes were embers in their sockets. 'As Grigori, we are part of the nine choirs of angels. Those of us who did not want to follow the path of our brethren, remained as Holy Watchers of the human kingdom from the spectrum of the rainbow.'

"I felt strangely pressured to leave and told them, 'Forgive me, but I hear my name. I must go.' I was conflicted, pulled in two directions, but the insistence from those calling my name overpowered me.

"'Return when the sunlight sprawls red across your horizon, and we will usher you farther into the other realms.' The white-haired one's harmonious voice was the last thing I heard." Elizabeth eased into consciousness from her reverie.

The story was recounted with authentic conviction. As Elizabeth became more alert, Antoinette watched her patient's eyes fasten on the crucifix that rose and fell on her chest with each breath she took.

Raw instincts thundered through the nun's gut and held her captive. "That is an extraordinary accounting, and I know you believe it to be true." Antoinette's tone was mildly patronizing.

Elizabeth's tale danced somewhere between the edges of life and afterlife and flirted with blasphemy. Elizabeth's story bordered on the forbidden, and the temptation to believe her was at Antoinette's door. The young woman had described two human prophets who lived exemplary lives and were among the less flawed ranks of archangels. She did not state their names, but if they did not end in "el," which meant "of God," they could be part of Satan's army. Antoinette would risk losing her own soul if she opened the door to learning more about these beings' intentions.

"I see the trays are out. It's almost dinnertime and you must be exhausted. We'll talk again in the morning." Antoinette observed how tranquil her patient now appeared.

Elizabeth repositioned her pillows and said, smiling, "Thank you for listening. There's more, but it can wait."

Antoinette crossed herself when she slipped out of the room and into the crowded hallway.

Chapter Six

Encounters

The hospital chapel was empty except for a petite elderly woman with a dowager's hump standing near the altar holding a wrinkled tissue to her eyes. Seeing the woman's crystal-beaded rosary between her gnarled fingers, Sister Antoinette approached her.

"May I be of assistance?" the nun asked.

"Oh, it's my husband. The doctors have told me they've done all they can, and I didn't know where else to turn." The woman's voice was weak and worn. "Help me to restore my faith, Sister."

"Have you lost your way? Come, let us pray together," Antoinette said, guiding the woman to a kneeling position in a pew near the front of the chapel. Head bent, touching her forehead to clasped hands resting on the pew in front of her, Antoinette spoke the verbal prayer, "Hail Mary, full of grace . . ."

After reciting the rosary prayer five times, she waited a respectable time before breaking the silence. "There, my dear, your prayers have been heard and may you have comfort knowing His loving kindness is with you. He hears us always and will not forsake you or your loved ones."

The woman dried her eyes, took both of the nun's hands in hers and thanked her. They embraced, and she made her way to the back of the chapel and left through the large oak door that led to the main hallway where it branched into patient care floors. After the woman's pale pink sweater disappeared from view, Antoinette struggled with her capacity to understand this woman's grief, or Elizabeth's, and prayed her God would inspire her and not abandon her.

Sister Antoinette had gone to the chapel to pray for Elizabeth's soul, and her own, because she suspected the beings of Elizabeth's dream might be the re-appearance of two of the hundred fallen Grigori angels she had learned about in seminary. Touted as mystical remnants from non-sanctioned texts and instruments of evil, the fallen ones consorted with humankind and delivered destructive instructions such as knowledge about tools of war. And, they produced half-breed giants with human women. Antoinette questioned God's judgment, and worse, His intent in placing them among the people. But, if the beings Elizabeth claimed to see were part of the band of Holy Watchers, the ones who remained God's highest emissaries who eluded religious lore, it would be revolutionary and she was determined to find out. She kneeled again and asked God for strength and wisdom to deliver effective counsel, and to lead Elizabeth to the true faith where her sins could be forgiven. After reciting the comforting chant of the rosary, Antoinette stood and quickly exited the chapel. Not wanting to be late for evening vespers, she made her way to the facility adjacent to the hospital where she lived.

❧ ❧ ❧

Elizabeth caught a glimpse of Marni holding a magnificent bouquet of amber-colored spider mums looking for room numbers in the hallway.

"Marni," Elizabeth called out and sat forward shoving her half-eaten meal on her dinner tray aside.

Marni drew her attention to the doorway and looked in and saw her friend. With tears in her eyes, she went straight to Elizabeth. Juggling the plant in her arms, they hugged and cried together.

"You look good, Liz, but I think you could use a cheeseburger and fries," Marni teased, glancing at the strips of dry turkey and cold mashed potatoes left on Elizabeth's plate. "God, it's good to see you awake," Marni said, holding her friend's hand. "I was here the first day, but you were still in the Twilight Zone."

"They tell me I'll be fine, but I'm tired. God, it's good to see you and the flowers—they're beautiful! You remembered about the mums." Tears bubbled up. "I'm sorry I put you through this, I don't know what to say—it's been confusing. This must have really messed things up for you. I know how much you had going at work, and I'm so sorry."

"I'm okay, it's you we've all been worried sick about. None of us realized—we thought you were getting over Stephen and on with life, but we should have known better. You had us fooled, Liz." The two women looked at each other, embraced again, and Marni sat in the bedside chair, hanging onto Elizabeth's hand.

"I've had incredible, unbelievable experiences, Marni." Elizabeth assessed her friend who was agnostic at best and she had to decide how much she would say. "You know I've literally returned from the dead."

"Let's not talk about it now. It'll keep. It's just so good to see you—well, so awake and together despite all that's happened. Yes, they told me it was a close call, and they had to revive you in the ambulance, your vitals were gone and . . ."

Elizabeth ignored Marni's attempt to deflect the subject of her near-death-experience and the two fell silent for a couple of moments.

"I'm not sure how to start, but a memory was triggered by those roses Doug sent," she said, gesturing toward the nightstand where the bouquet of American Beauties radiated their award-winning color. "Two beings led me into a garden overflowing with red flowers, and, well, they were actually angels. They told me the color red's frequency is a gateway to the Grigori angels who are the ancient Holy Watchers who dwell in the fifth dimension in the color bands of rainbows. God, Marni, it was surreal." Elizabeth lay back against her propped up pillows.

Marni looked at her friend who seemed to believe she had ventured into some netherworld experience. The faraway look in Elizabeth's pale gray eyes peered into another dimension.

Marni fidgeted, and let go of her friend's hand. After Elizabeth's divulgence, Marni got up and fussed with straightening bedclothes and tried to change the subject again by talking to her friend as if she was still strung out on the drugs she had consumed. "Let's talk about this after you've had a chance to rest more and get a little stronger. Have you talked to Doug yet?

Having his own law practice must not allow for much flexibility."

"He's made arrangements to stay and help me out. Actually, he's due back this evening. I suspect he'll try to talk me into going to L.A. for a while," she said, her voice trailing off.

Marni brightened. "You could stay with me, Liz. I'm sure Rizbah wouldn't mind, although she'd probably snoop through every inch of your belongings."

"I can hold my own with that old fur ball," Elizabeth smiled, remembering the feisty feline that ran Marni's household. "She'd be great company, but I don't know—"

"Well, you don't have to decide anything for a while. You know I'd do anything to help. Oh, and don't worry about your house. I tidied up, dumped the perishables from the fridge, got your mail and hauled out the trash so it's habitable. Did they say when you'll be getting out of here?" Marni asked.

"Not sure, but they unhooked me from everything today, so I can navigate on my own now. Soon, I suspect. They said I need a psych consult, so I'll have to go through that before they release me."

Marni, uncomfortable with such clinical details, nervously opened her purse and cleared her throat. "I almost forgot. Uh, everyone from the agency sends their best," she said, pulling out a card and a frayed hardbound copy of *One Hundred and One Famous Poems* and handed them to her friend. "We all signed this. I thought you might like to have something to read—I found this on your nightstand."

"How thoughtful. You're sweet, Marn." Elizabeth extracted the card from its envelope and read it. "I don't know if I can ever face . . . I'm so embarrassed. Please thank everybody for thinking of me." She stood the card upright on the side table.

An orderly entered the room, picked up the dinner tray with its dried remains, and left.

Marni got up and slung her black saddlebag purse over her shoulder, indicating she was ready to leave. "I've stayed too long—I know you need to chill. Have Doug give me a call, if you want anything from the house. I can pack some clothes and toiletries and bring them by tomorrow. Give some thought about staying with me. If I can help you work this out, I'm here for you."

Elizabeth smiled and said, "I will. Thank you for everything. I love the card and flowers! My best to the crew. When I figure out what's going on, we'll talk." She tapped her phone on the bedside table. They hugged hard, squeezing hands good-bye and Marni disappeared through the doorway, glancing back at her friend.

Both women were left to think about all that was left unsaid.

Chapter Seven

The Land of Rainbows

Elizabeth sat by the window wrapped in a white-cotton robe like a moth in a cocoon. She watched a reluctant sun bathe the mid-morning in soft autumn light. Her thoughts were focused on the psych meeting she had earlier. The matronly doctor arranged for anti-depressant drug therapy and a series of counseling appointments. The first one was scheduled next week.

Elizabeth turned toward the door when she saw Antoinette briskly approaching. She warmly said, "Good morning, Sister." Elizabeth imagined Antoinette's faith was genuine, but wondered why she was so attentive to a non-Catholic, much less a person who attempted suicide, the worst sin of all. The thought that she was going to try and convert her bubbled up with a ring of truth.

"It's wonderful seeing you up and out of bed." Peering out the window in the direction Elizabeth had been staring she said, "Autumn skies are like no others." She studied Elizabeth's face. "I understand you saw Dr. Cooper this morning for assessment?" she asked, eying Elizabeth over the tops of the lenses balanced in the middle of her fleshy nose.

"Her questions brought up a lot of old stuff, but I felt okay talking about it." She re-arranged the folds of her housecoat over her knees.

"May I sit with you? It seems we need to finish our talk, if you feel up to it." Not waiting for Elizabeth to respond, Antoinette scooted a chair next to her with a raspy screech.

"I've been thinking. It's all I can do to not to think about everything that's happened. I feel different, relieved, well, maybe that's not the right word." Elizabeth picked at a hangnail then shifted her attention to Antoinette. "Why do I interest you, Sister?" Elizabeth didn't miss it when the nun winced at her words.

"As you said, dear, you have taken away an extraordinary memory from a traumatic ordeal, and I'm curious about it. I know something about the angelic realms and I would like to learn more about your experience." Antoinette straightened her back and breathed from the upper shallows of her chest, wearing a reverent expression and lowering her eyes.

"Your story might restore faith to another who may be in doubt or despair. To know these good angels exist would be a spiritual gift."

Elizabeth was ready to reclaim her reverie, and put her suspicions in abeyance. She softly closed her eyes and allowed herself to lapse into the memory of her encounter. "The beings I told you about, the ones I met in the red garden, told me I had the choice to leave and return to my body, to my life here, but that I could re-enter their world again by concentrating on the color red, any red object would do. Before I woke up in this room, the angels assured me I owned the memory of my entire journey into the rainbow realms."

Sister Antoinette said a barely audible prayer for the protection of both their souls before Elizabeth began.

"The dark one, who called himself Metatron, met me against the backdrop of a sunset where we slipped over the crimson threshold to find the white-haired one waiting for us. Metatron spoke in his distinctive operatic baritone, 'We are the Qaddisin, the twin Holy Watchers, who oversee the color bands and are known as the highest Orders of angels.' Their strong physical contrasts made it hard to believe they were related, but their unified light was brilliant and poured out the same fierce magnetic power. I could feel it—like I was sitting on the edge of a long silver sword moving headlong and it would slice me in half. I followed behind them at a cautious distance down a narrow passageway. We drew closer and floated through to the opening at the end where a warm blush glowed and grew larger. On the other side were fields of bright poppies surrounding a great mound dotted with Moorish-style temples constructed of burnished copper and bronze ablaze with the radiance of the atmosphere.

"Metatron spoke, 'We have entered the orange frequency, Elizabeth. You are here by divine appointment and have a covenant that you fulfill your destiny when you return to Earth. You will learn about The Holy Watchers of this color band who are sanctioned to observe humankind's emotions. It is one of the most important and demanding vocations of the Orders.' His dark eyes traced a map across my face.

"Twirling in unison, the twins moved forward toward the closest structure, and I willed myself to follow. Marveling at the massive copper dome dwarfing us, I was intrigued with the scale of the architecture, its multiple doors, windows and passageways that punctuated the seamless surface of its walls. Round turrets spiraled around the edge of the dome giving the occupants a panoramic view. Nearing the entrance, fear and excitement flip-flopped in my stomach. The Qaddisin disappeared to my left through a double doorway. I skirted sharply around the massive doorframe and saw they had entered a room with hundreds of beings in uniform velvet capes the color of Spanish oranges. Illuminated charts and tables sprawled in every direction and clusters of light beings gathered around every available workspace. Our entrance did not distract them.

"'Come, Elizabeth. We want to show you how we oversee the emotional world.' The twin with white hair and enormous height invited me over, looking regal in crimson silk. 'You may call me Sandalphon.'

"I drifted over and joined them at a round table the size of the Hubble telescope lens.

"The illusion of a three-dimensional Earth, rose up from the surface creating a relief map-like image I was tempted to touch. Its brilliant colors flashed and shifted and Sandalphon pointed a tapered artisan's finger toward areas that were "hotter" than others; ones that were blinking fiery pinpoints of light. Several regions were clustered and pulsating. 'These groupings are magnified on smaller tables and are watched by angels at stations here and throughout this complex, Elizabeth. They represent the "hot spots" of humanity and bear serious surveillance. We are primed to intervene, if there is imbalance in their activity and are called upon to mitigate.' I ran my mind down the laundry list of places in the world that would qualify for crucial observation points.

"Metatron chimed in, 'And it is not confined to global geographical aspects. Within every relationship there is the potential for unbalanced emotions, both positive and negative at war with each other.' He must have sensed my thoughts, because my mind considered the conflicts encountered in everyday life—such as being cut off in traffic or arguing about who takes out the trash. I had not weighed the value of emotions in its role in the scheme of life before.

"'You must have questions?' Metatron asked politely.

"'I'm overwhelmed at the implications,' I said, as I swept my gaze over the enormous globe. 'The enormity and scope of the work here is endless. Do you monitor individuals as well as groups of people in these communities and countries?'

"Looking sidelong at me, Metatron responded, 'Even before humankind was created we knew one of our missions would be to watch over the passions and emotions of creation, since humanity is a catalyst for both constructive and destructive ends.' I was strangely comforted by his words and believed it referred to their intervention in my circumstances. My emotions surrounding Stephen's death had suffocated me, and they must have been glowing like hot coals on the screens in the orange realm for months.

"Two auburn-clad angels drifted over and consulted the map during our exchange, but never acknowledged our presence. Their bronze capes were made from the old pile-cut type of fabric whose sheen could not be rivaled by modern synthetics. My guides nodded their heads signaling it was time to leave the main chamber. Their filmy red silk garments wafted behind them, as they took the lead and left the room leaving me to follow once again in their ephemeral wake.

"Outside the pavilion I saw Metatron and Sandalphon pause on a knoll at the edge of a poppy field. I continued to marvel at the ease of my mobility, as I floated and joined them in a soundless movement without the sensation of my feet touching the ground. Carved amber chairs and benches sat atop the hard-packed clay ground. With a sweep of their hands, they invited me to sit and rest.

"'You are keeping up well, Elizabeth. You were right about the intervention. Yes, we saw your light and rescued you from your own hand, because you needed to be shown it did not have to be your time to exit the Earth. There is great potential in your future and there is much work for you to accomplish,' Sandalphon said, his voice a melody.

"'I wonder if I can ever feel whole without Stephen by my side. I don't believe I can manage life without him. You must have seen his magnificent light withdraw from that table when he died,' I said sadly. Barely audible, Metatron responded, 'We did. That's how we knew to watch you more intently.' I couldn't meet his eyes, but looked down on the coppery soil and gave thanks in the shadow of silence."

Chapter Eight

Pure Gold

"When I looked up, I saw both Sandalphon and Metatron with indescribable expressions of compassion on their faces. A wash of unconditional love rippled over me and any sense of time and space dissolved. It registered that my entry into their realm was a privileged passage. A faint glimmer shone from their chests and connected with my heart. Since Stephen's death, I'd missed that sensation of unconditional love and I let theirs fill the void.

"Metatron broke the spell. 'The golden kingdom is connected to the heart where universal love exists. Its energy created you.' Motioning toward a bright spot on the horizon, he said, 'There is the land of gold—where all matters of the heart are watched.'

"I let the idea that I'd entered an enchanted limbo sink in. Where each realm of color was populated with angels that presided over the complexities of human life. This magical arena surpassed anything my artist's imagination could create.

"Sandalphon's white skin and hair created the perfect frame for his aquamarine eyes. 'The land of green lies beyond these meadows of daffodils and the golden city of the heart. Its vibration complements the verdant ribbon that pulsates with healing energy.' The two beings allowed me to rest and absorb their heart energies and digest their revelations. 'The calm will prepare you for the intensity of the vibration within the yellow band,' Metatron almost whispered in his deep voice.

"A sea of bright flowers grew in the fields that surrounded another knoll.

A light breeze tilted the buttery faces of the blooms, and when they swayed, their rhythms performed a hypnotic dance. I was acutely aware of my companions and I savored feeling their love—something for which I had hungered the past few months.

"A thin white hand and firm dark one touched each of mine and I ascended from the translucent bench. Without effort, we journeyed through the waves of daffodils swaying in the wind. Their subtle scent perfumed the air. We maneuvered ourselves headlong toward the distant glow, a halo, where the band of color met the open sky.

"In a blink, we lit upon a thin sheet of shining gold that sprawled before us and paved the way into a village. An ethereal haze emanated from a natural formation of crystals that were hollowed out to create structures and form the city. My companions had not fully prepared me for the potent energy that poured into me, as we wafted through the golden streets. They hovered close to me and made frequent eye contact. 'You could not have fully prepared me for this,' I said, with an awestruck smile.

"The maze of streets and alleyways took us into the central core of the metropolis where an enormous carved citrine dome blazed and dazzled my eyes and consciousness. I could see circles of brilliant canary diamonds encrusted around portholes from which shafts of light poured.

"'Elizabeth,' Sandalphon said, 'this is the cosmic Temple of Love situated in the heart of the yellow realm. Here all human life sprinkled throughout the cosmos is infused with the capability to give and receive love. It is the universal source of the holy connection and configuration of transcendent love.' He swept his beautiful hand toward the structure. 'One of the highest orders of angels coordinate this significant hub of the universe.'

"'Can we go inside?' I asked, unable to fathom what the force of energy was like within the dome's matrix.

"'Certainly, but you will emerge transformed by its power and be molecularly rearranged to your original state—to that time before your emotions altered the purity of your existence,' Metatron warned in his imperial voice. I nodded I was ready, and with a deep visceral breath, I opened myself to its promise.

"My guides escorted me to the commanding arched entrance framed with twinkling facets of gemstones. A convex door three times my height was seamlessly cut from the stone of the dome. Metatron inserted his hand into a notch carved into its glassy surface and pulled the door toward him. Immediately, golden light streamed out onto me, its warmth penetrating my body. Sandalphon led the way, my hand in Metatron's who eased me over the threshold.

"A shimmering globe suspended over a ring of glistening citrine crystals dominated the room. Spokes of sparkling sun-colored stones fanned out from the circle of crystals to chambers in the perimeter of the semi-spherical roof. As it was in the orange band, I saw angels at work at their celestial missions. Androgynous honey-haired beings in metallic gold tunics focused on regulating the minute specks of light that filtered down from the great orb into channels that flowed to the anterooms.

"Through the transparent walls of crystalline sheared into thin sheets that formed each of the rooms at the end of the fiery spokes, I could see more angelic beings examining pods of light. Magically, they converted them into a laser stream that projected into the ethers through the circular diamond-ringed windows I'd noticed when we approached the dome.

"Hovering near the Mother Light, I tingled and drank in its benevolent purity. Its aura washed every molecule in my body and enfolded me in its power. After basking in the charged energy, Metatron and Sandalphon broke my reverie by gently guiding me toward the massive entrance door where we smoothly exited the exquisite dome. I could feel the muscles in my face relax into a mask of bliss, as the effects of the light continued their work."

Chapter Nine

The Healing Realm

"My hosts escorted me along the golden foot path toward another trail leading us away from the Temple. We passed more crystalline structures, but now lush outcroppings of vegetation dotted the spaces among them.

"'How are you feeling, Elizabeth?' Sandalphon asked.

"'Unlike I ever have before. There are no words to describe the peace and sense of wholeness, Sandalphon. I feel safe and comforted, as if cradled in loving arms.' My voice surprised me—it was soft, reverent, and I caught my companions exchanging glances that betrayed their complicity in my transformation.

"'Your heart was in need of remembering its source,' Metatron uttered. They drifted ahead, their garments brushing my face as they passed.

"Pea-size chunks of gravel littered the metallic passage that led away from the crystal city. As we ambled over the golden surface, more pebbles and rocks appeared and grassy tufts sprouted around the shimmering foil's thinning edges. The road unraveled into a vast sea of grass that sloped into a long deep valley. Plush forests surrounded the emerald expanse and stark majestic peaks rose behind the abundant swell of evergreens.

"The fragrant meadow was an invitation to rest after the powerful experience in the dome. As if my companions knew my longings, they veered in unison to a small round hilltop sheltered by a stand of white birches. Two red splashes of color settled behind the screen of white bark and waited for me.

"'This landscape reminds me of a childhood fantasy,' I said, sweeping up the slope and perching at the feet of Sandalphon. 'My dad took me to the redwood forests once, and I always imagined I'd return to those groves of great trees, so aromatic and cool. I'd picture myself walking beneath them, spilling my troubles, and the trees and earth would quietly absorb all the pain of whatever the crisis was. It was a comforting ritual that got me through many childhood hurts. Life is not meant for those who are sensitive.' I shot them a look that revealed my humanness.

"'This is the green zone, Elizabeth—the place of rejuvenation, and growth. When the earthly agonies in body, mind or soul cry out in prayer or desperation, the angel spirits who live in the fertile valleys and timbered mountains transmit the green band energies to all in need. Healing does not appear to be happening at times, but it always is manifesting at some level.' Sandalphon looked at me like a loving parent. 'Perhaps you visited this kingdom in your childhood musings.'

"Sandalphon's luminous eyes penetrated mine. 'Just as they do in the forests here, spritely angels populate the green belts on Earth. When you return, look under a leaf or pine bough and you might find one ready to help you through any difficult time.' His whole face twinkled. 'The legends and lore about leprechauns and pixies in the land of Erin must be true,' I responded with a wink.

"Metatron remained quiet, preoccupied, never taking his gaze from the craggy horizon. We slipped into his mood and fell silent, listening to the sounds of the forest and leaves rustling overhead. The unconditional love I felt beating in my chest buoyed the imposing view and beauty that surrounded us. I wanted to stay forever.

"Inaudible communication broke our reverie. We rose together, as easy as breathing, and propelled our forms down the knoll and traveled farther into the valley. Giant ferns, conifer forests and magnificent foliage proliferated in every direction, and I was awed by the profound silence it created. I drifted off the path a few times to peek under a leaf or behind a bush, but never found one of the little green angels camouflaged in their realm. But I believed they were there.

"In the distance at the edge of the green band, I saw the trees thin and promise another clearing where the sky opened and changed from a clear sunlit blue to the deepest shades in the spectrum.

"Metatron anticipated my musings about our passage into the next color band. 'Yes, we will soon enter the noble etheric realms of blue and indigo—and beyond that lies the band of the violet flame, the pure white light and the ultimate Elohim. They are the highest of earthly connections to spirit and are the harbingers of your celestial royalty, Elizabeth.'

"With that, an expanse widened before us, and we emerged from the forests. I halted, speechless at what I saw."

Chapter Ten

Down to Earth

Elizabeth and Antoinette were silhouettes against the hospital window filled with a cool blue sky. The nun's attention was riveted on her patient, as if bewitched. Antoinette quietly shifted her weight within the confines of the rigid chair, but did not interrupt Elizabeth's flow of concentration. The nun held her breath and cross unconsciously, as the revelations unfolded.

Without warning, Elizabeth's eyes fluttered open, as she returned to the conscious world. Antoinette camouflaged her disappointment by using her most affected tone, "You're so serene, my dear. So at peace. Much better than when we first started. How are you feeling?"

"I'm well, Sister, thank you. There's much more. I'm starting to remember what I saw, how it felt, what I knew. It's hard to describe—" Elizabeth massaged her face and eyes awake, stretching her arms in front of her, letting go of the thread of memory that held Antoinette's attention.

Excusing herself, she crossed Antoinette's line of vision. Unsure of her footing, she made her way measuredly to the bathroom, holding the backs of chairs, mules sliding across the polished floor. Inside, she looked at her reflection in a narrow mirror above the sink protruding from the wall. A pale, but ageless face looked back. Was she altered in some way from the recollection of her rainbow journey among great archangels? Turning on the hot water, and squirting a dab of antibacterial soap onto her palm, she worked up a lather to wash her face. She would forever tie the scent of the soap to her salvation from suicide and the days that followed in the hospital. She rinsed and rubbed the coarse towel across her skin restoring the color that had been missing. Her hands still damp, she smoothed loose strands of hair and assessed her image, daring to look into her eyes for the first time in several days. Had she changed? Looked different? In some indefinable way, she knew she was.

Antoinette checked her watch. Elizabeth's amazing account was nested inside her to digest. Its implications churned and dredged up questions for the nun and every aspect of what it implied was jarring. But it was a secret gift for her to pray over, or take out and contemplate when challenges arose in her inexplicable world of the hospital and spiritual life.

When Elizabeth emerged from the bathroom, Antoinette said, "You look revived, dear. Nice to see you freshened up." The acts of tidying her hair and washing her face were healthy, symbolic gestures that anchored her in the present.

The nun got on her feet by popping loose from the chair's grip. "I suspect your brother will be here before long to handle the arrangements regarding your discharge, and I'm afraid I've neglected my other patients. I will look in on you this evening and perhaps you will be up to finishing your extraordinary story, then?" Antoinette's eyes narrowed.

Antoinette withdrew in her efficient manner with her trademark rustle of skirts. The brightness of the sky poured into the room and made Elizabeth squint in its gathering glare, as she returned to bed. Still wearing the lightweight robe, she maneuvered under the coverlet and made herself as comfortable as possible and picked up the worn book of poetry Marni brought. As she had done since childhood, she let the pages drop open randomly. The selection often contained an appropriate passage to fit her situation and mood. Her eyes fell on a line from Longfellow's, "A Psalm of Life," and the irony penetrated.

There were major life decisions to be made, and yet, after recounting her visitation with the rainbow dwellers to Sister Antoinette, the urgency to continue her life in the same way lessened. The aura of a new-found peace buoyed her from the pressures that weighed so heavily just a few days before. Replaced by a sense of purpose that stirred inside of her, she held an understanding that a roadmap of her life was yet to unfold.

Mid-afternoon shadows fell across the room. Douglas Potter found Elizabeth sitting up in bed reading. Her face brightened, seeing this man who had been a brother more by circumstance of birth than a true sibling relationship. He had always been tall and thin, but she now observed that he carried a small paunch underneath his beige pullover sweater. His love for looking natty had not changed and she detected strands of gray in the close-cropped sandy-colored hair that had noticeably thinned. Eight years separated them—he was nearly out of the house by the time she had gathered many memories of their motherless life together.

"Liz," Doug went to her and leaned over to embrace her, "I'm so glad to see you awake, uh, and more yourself, I mean, I wasn't sure what to expect."

"I understand. I'm okay. Really. I'm so sorry to have put you through this."

"My God, you gave us a scare." He sat down on the bed and took her hand, looking intently into her face.

"Doug. I wasn't thinking beyond myself and never intended to have you and Jenna involved in my problems. I just wanted out—I couldn't go on without Stephen." Doug pulled her up and hugged her. Both had tears in their eyes. She relaxed back down on her pillows.

"What matters is that you are going to get better, and you don't have to do it alone. Right? I didn't realize how hard you took Stephen's death, not really. I want to make it up to you. We owe it to ourselves to get to know each other better." Doug looked down, repositioned his feet on the newly polished tile and clenched his jaw to quell a knot of emotion. "I hardly know you, really know you, Liz. It's about time we tried to become a family. Dad always wanted this, and it should have happened. I didn't take the time or make much effort. This is a wake-up call, as far as I am concerned. Having nearly lost you, I realize that we have shared few memories."

Elizabeth reached out and pulled him to her again, hugging him hard. They let tears trace marks on their cheeks. "It wasn't all you, Doug. I felt I was in your way. You were always so goal-oriented and driven." He smiled an acknowledging response, and held up his hands as if to say, guilty. Elizabeth continued, "I could have made more of an effort. My life was wrapped up in my career and Stephen and time got away. I always thought it might be better that way, since your life was so different from mine."

They filled the remainder of the day catching up on the silent years that stood between them. Official visiting hours were nearly over. A nurse made her rounds and poked her head in, saying she would check back.

"Oh, and thank you for the beautiful roses, Doug. They helped me remember an incredible experience I had when I was unconscious. I need and want to tell you about it sometime." Elizabeth's voice tightened with urgency.

"I'm staying at the downtown Marriott." He reached into his coat pocket for a business card. "Here's my cell number, if you need to call for any reason. I'll be in after rush hour in the morning to take care of your paperwork—they told me you were ready to be discharged tomorrow." Doug's expression softened in relief and he handed her the card. "And I want you to think about coming to stay with Jenna and me for a while. God knows, we have the room. I know L.A. isn't your thing, but I think time and space away from the memories and connection to Stephen might help, and be good for all of us." Doug's voice carried the strong conviction and timbre of an attorney's practiced persuasion skills.

The evening shift floor nurse returned, Doug rose and kissed his sister good night on the forehead. As he crossed the room's threshold, he heard Elizabeth's response.

"All right, Doug, I'll think about it."

Chapter Eleven

The Return

Elizabeth leaned back on the fine charcoal-colored leather of the rental car's plush seat and glanced at Doug's profile that was a stronger version of hers. He still liked upscale cars and looked completely natural maneuvering the silver Mercedes sedan through late morning traffic. Her head still felt light and foggy at times, but she was relieved to be out of the hospital and headed home. She had mixed feelings about returning to her house. In one way she felt like a failure and dreaded the old emotional charge of seeing reminders of Stephen. But she was also grateful not to have to be doing it alone and was curious how this reunion with her brother would play out. She regretted not seeing Sister Antoinette last night and there was so much going on this morning, they only had a brief exchange. She wanted to offer a proper good-bye and thank her for her caring and support, no matter her motives. Elizabeth made a mental commitment to visit her later when she felt stronger and finish telling Antoinette the rest of her vision or experience, since she had expressed a genuine interest.

"Did you eat much this morning? Would you like to stop for take-out, coffee? You probably haven't had a decent cup in weeks. Should be about an hour before we get to your place according to Ms. GPS here," he said, patting the console. "Or we can stop at the store first and get some essentials. You'll have to do that anyway."

"Let's go home first and I can see what I'll need. Marni said she cleared out a lot of stuff since she didn't know how long I'd be gone. Oh, Doug, she's been an incredible friend—an angel in the storm and I owe her a lot," Elizabeth's chin dropped to her chest overcome with gratitude.

A stoplight changed to green, and Doug turned onto the expressway's ramp. "It would be great if you would go back to L.A. with me. Jenna insists it would be a chance to do girl things, sister things. Have an opportunity to bond, as they say."

"You're a good salesman, brother, but for now, I don't know what I want. It may be a while until I feel up to speed." Elizabeth's soft voice seemed to have lost strength from yesterday.

"You might change your mind," Doug encouraged with a smile in his voice. "At least, we hope so. I'm going with you said you'd think about it."

The countryside sped by in a surreal blur, as the Mercedes shot down the four-lane highway. Doug followed the articulated GPS directions, and commented on the gorgeous autumn blaze that clung to the trees. Otherwise, they drove in silence, and Elizabeth closed her eyes and dozed, lulled by the hum of tires on pavement and the vehicle's flawless ride.

"Welcome back, did you have a good snooze?" Doug reached over and tugged on a strand of her fine hair.

Elizabeth looked up from her nap feeling groggy, but refreshed, too.

"I can see why you love it here—nothing like New England in the fall. The air alone is worth the trip. "After this turnoff, what is the best way to get to your house? Sometimes directions from the locals are better."

"Just follow the signs to New Bristol and turn right at the first stop light—it's a few miles from there."

Remnants of fiery leaves were piled in yards and swirled into clumps that clogged gutters and sewer drains. Elizabeth's heart started to race in her chest, as he veered onto her street. She never imagined that she would see her house again. Pulling into the driveway, nothing on the outer had changed, but the whole of her interior world had been transformed. Elizabeth knew her decision to go home was the right one, as long as Doug was with her. She had to grapple with the challenges of the reminders, the memories of life without Stephen before she could move on. Suppressing the grief and rage led her to this situation. Her learning on this earth was far from over. She considered it was for some unknown reason that she survived. And with the medication, counseling support and her mystical memory of the beautiful angels and their realms, she was in a different mental and physical space.

Doug opened the trunk and retrieved the luggage Marni had packed earlier in the week and his own black garment bag and carry-on. Elizabeth was bundled up in a zippered fuzzy rose-colored lounge robe Doug brought to her that morning. He placed the small valise in her lap, unzipped it and waited while Elizabeth found her purse and rummaged through it. She retrieved her keys, then he helped her to her feet and they made their way to the quaint 1920s-style bungalow with its glassed-in porch. With a deep breath, she placed the heart-shaped brass key into the lock. She was home.

After Doug settled her onto the couch and plumped a comforter around her, he turned up the thermostat and Elizabeth thought it smelled dry after being turned off for so many days. Doug found the kitchen and quickly assessed the food situation. It was clear he knew his way around a pantry and quickly got the water to boil and prepared tea. He shouted out the inventory remaining in her fridge and cabinets above the main countertop.

Elizabeth thought, where did he learn all this? She smiled inwardly, never having had the opportunity to see much of his domestic side. It must come from having kids. She sobered at the thought of children, as she mourned the thought of never having them herself.

"You need the works, Liz. Marni was thorough! Is there anything special you feel like before I go? Plenty of canned goods—maybe some soup?" He was working hard to be upbeat and casual, but there was an edge in his voice.

"I like to have cheese as my go-to snack. Maybe Swiss and colby-jack and a sliced muenster? All the salad stuff, too. Did you find any crackers? If not, anything wheat's okay. I'll need 1% milk and eggs, and lemon yogurt sounds good, but no store brands. Remember when we used to flip a coin over the last piece of coconut cream pie? Buzzuto's downtown has a great deli and bakery—you'll find a good one there. How about a loaf of dill rye? A loaf of that or anything else you see would be good." Elizabeth surprised herself being able to think about food with a measure of enthusiasm for the first time since Stephen's death.

Doug returned to the living room placing a steaming cup of peppermint tea on a woven coaster near the edge of the coffee table. Elizabeth's mood presented as too light, but since he was skeptical by profession and nature, he questioned her. "Are you sure you're okay to be alone a while?" He watched his sister carefully as he retrieved the remote and her phone and laid them next to the tea, before he went to the bedroom for an extra pillow.

"I'll be fine. Really. I've had a lot of time to prepare for this re-entry. I won't do anything stupid." She smiled convincingly at her brother. "I'll check in with Marni and let her know I'm home. After you leave Sunday, she wanted me to spend a few weeks at her place until I feel like being here alone on my own. I'll know by Sunday whether that's the plan. I have the Goldstein's next door for a safety net until they leave next month. Please try to be patient. Nothing's clear, but I feel better and have to take it a day at a time."

"This shouldn't take long." Doug picked up her cell and added his number to her contacts list. "In case you think of something else or need anything. Sure you'll be okay?"

Elizabeth's confusion and inability to make decisions were red flags for Doug, but his mission was to return to L.A. with her. There was something to be said for Elizabeth's ability to make a living in this small community where lifestyles were infinitely less complex and intense, but it might propel her back into the depression. Grabbing his jacket, Doug gave her a thumb's up, and was out the glass-paned door, headed for the grocery store and Buzzuto's.

Elizabeth considered filling the house with noisy news of the outside world, but laid down the remote and scanned the room and remembered her last night here. The memory was vivid, as she had planned her suicide ritual carefully. It was both terrifying and surreal, and being back in the house she thought she'd never see again increased her anxiety. She sipped her tea, and recalled the endless amount of time it took to swallow the pills, the last-minute panic and fear that nearly strangled her and then the plateau where she experienced a place of surrender and resolve to follow through with it. That's how it was. She had a surge of regret, but by then it was too late as lethargy set in before she slipped into sleep, a deep blissful sleep. The room was the same, nothing had changed. The same familiar photographs of her and Stephen, their books crammed into charming built-in cabinets that lined the room and her egg collection in the antique mahogany curio cabinet were exactly as she left them. She was able to look at these things in a new light—one that was tender, but different now. They belonged to the past which was meant to be treasured. Had she only known that Stephen was not really gone, but that he and the angels awaited her within the folds of rainbows.

Picking up her phone, Elizabeth punched in Marni's number and listened to its familiar old-fashioned ring tone. Fridays were usually busy with deadlines at the office, so she let it ring several times until the voice mail clicked on and Elizabeth left her message.

"Hi, it's Liz. I'm home."

Chapter Twelve

Considerations

Liz ran water in the claw-footed tub until steam clouded the tall beveled mirror above the freestanding sink. After leaving her fuzzy robe in a pile on the floor, she swiped her hand across the water. Satisfied it was not too hot, she stepped in and descended into the soothing warmth.

Lying submerged in the scented water, she thought about how Stephen used to join her in the bath after a long day. She reflected on the sweetness of their intimate moments and it evoked a hotbed of tears from that mercurial well of grief, dragging her into the familiar dark tunnel. With self-talk, she climbed out of the hole and the emotions passed. She shifted her thoughts to what life might be like away from all of this, away from the house, its associations and eroded dreams. The California scene never resonated, but to miss an opportunity to get to know Doug and Jenna better, and her niece and nephew, Channing and Jackson, was something to weigh carefully. But she wasn't ready to think about that now. "Be in the present moment," she could hear the doctor's words in her head, but bringing them into her heart was another matter. Elizabeth forced herself to concentrate on the healing properties of the water that restored and leeched out the muscle aches that was a result of lying in bed for too many days. Eventually, her thoughts slowed and meandered toward the experience of the angelic crystalline world of The Watchers where she felt absolute peace.

The phone buzzed like an alarm clock that jolted her awake. She grabbed it from the stool beside the tub and it nearly slipped out of her wet hands.

"Hey, sis, did I wake you?"

"I'm just soaking in a tub. I must have drifted off."

"I'm ready to check out and wondered if you'd like me to pick up a pizza and we could watch a movie and just chill out. Okay with you?"

Elizabeth smiled. The idea of simple pleasures and Doug's thoughtfulness warmed her. "Couldn't think of anything better. Did you get a red wine?"

"Good idea. See you." He added playfully, "Ciao."

She tapped the off button on the cell and rose out of the water. Toweling off, she padded to the bedroom and donned jeans and a corduroy shirt then headed to the kitchen to check if Marni left the condiments at least. Opening the fridge, she scanned the side door and took out a bottle of Tabasco sauce wondering if Doug liked it on pizza like she did.

≥• ≥• ≥•

The last of the movie the credits scrolled down the screen and Doug turned the set off and said, "I haven't seen *Picnic* in years. What a window on mid-century values. Just before the shift to the '60s culture. What do you think happens to Kim Novak? Maybe she returns home or was the bad boy, William Holden, her true love?" Doug enjoyed the analysis. "He was just too old for her."

"It was definitely another era. I'm glad we are where we are now at least from a woman's point of view! I think it was all about lust. They had a definite toxic chemistry, but to give up an easier life where she was a big fish in a little pond? I don't know." Elizabeth wrinkled her nose.

"If you could finish the story, how would you do it?" Doug asked.

Elizabeth shrugged and considered for a moment. "I'm all about happy endings. Life isn't necessarily like that." Tears started to well.

Doug changed the direction of the conversation. "Well, I think it worked out. She took a risk, and followed her heart. It wasn't like that for Jenna and me. I mean, she wasn't interested at all at first. Took me two months to get her to go out with me." Doug shook his head remembering. The pizza box lay open with half eaten slices and strips of crust. He flipped the lid closed over the remnants, and emptied the last of the wine into his glass.

"How did you and Jenna meet? There's so much I don't know."

"One of my associates at the law firm. His wife was taking a Pilates class from her and he thought we'd hit it off and we did, but I had to exercise every bit of charm I had," Doug's eyes twinkled.

"No doubt you did. Sometimes it's better to be friends first, don't you think? Stephen and I were like that." Elizabeth pulled her knees to her chest and rested her head on them then looked up at her brother. "I appreciate all you've done, Doug. It's amazing that we hardly know each other, but here we are." She uncurled herself, sat cross-legged in her chair. "By the way, I knew you'd like Tabasco on your pizza. Dad must have started it or at least we can decide he's responsible for the tradition." Elizabeth gazed into the last of the red wine in her glass. Memories bubbled up. Images of Metatron's claret-colored robe surfaced and she let them overtake her. She nearly slipped into a trance.

"Hey, Lizzy, you okay?" Doug asked. He leaned forward in her direction. He checked her eyes and pulse to make sure she was not having a reaction to the meds combined with the one glass of wine she nursed all evening.

Elizabeth popped her head up and saw Doug looking at her with a concerned expression.

"It feels like I'm processing enough stuff to fill the Library of Congress. Sorry. You must have a million questions." She shifted her position and straightened her back inviting a deep stretch.

"I do, but none that can't wait. Let's relax and let it unravel naturally in the next few days. For tonight, I'm willing to put the heavy items on a shelf. We're navigating uncharted waters we've never sailed together before, but if this is what it took to bring us together, then I know something good will come from it, Liz." He moved closer and raised his glass. "To new beginnings." The delicate crystal clinked with a pure bell-like sound and each took a decent sip.

Chapter Thirteen

Sister Antoinette

Doug circled around a packed parking lot several times before stopping at the front entrance to drop off his sister. He said, "You wait inside while I find a parking place. I see a bench in the entry and I'll meet you there."

Elizabeth had more energy this morning, as she peeled out of the car. She turned and waved at him before she approached the giant automated glass doors.

Inside, Elizabeth positioned herself on the foyer bench, unbuttoned her coat and pulled her phone from her purse. She checked her messages and there were two from Marni and one from the office. Her messages were reminders to check in and that she had procrastinated and was being pressed to make decisions. Doug would be with her to help with appointments and getting a routine started and then he would be gone. Her option to stay with Marni after Doug left meant she could always be with her family later. A familiar voice interrupted her texting her responses.

"My dear, Elizabeth."

Sister Antoinette had entered her peripheral vision.

The nun quickly scrutinized her. Spending time with family played a major role in the restoration of a patient's health and Elizabeth was no exception.

Elizabeth clasped Antoinette's outstretched hand, as she joined her on the bench. "I'm waiting for my brother to park. Thank you, again, for your kindness and patience."

"No need for any of that. Family time appears to agree with you. What brings you here today?" she asked with a barb on her words.

"Paperwork and I'm meeting with a therapist to set up a schedule for the next few months."

"Hmm, I see. Perhaps when you feel able, stronger, we can set up a time to finish our conversation?" She evaluated Elizabeth's face.

"Remind me—I am not sure where we left off—I was a little groggy."

"You were telling me about the dream you had." Sister Antoinette cast her eyes on a crucifix on the opposite wall.

"Well, I'm not sure it was a dream," Elizabeth offered cautiously.

The whoosh of doors opening and gush of icy air accompanied Doug, as he approached the women on the bench. "Do you ever get used to this cold?" Doug asked as he shivered.

Elizabeth and Antoinette stood.

"Doug, this is Sister Antoinette. She's been very kind and looked after me here." Doug's tall frame dwarfed the nun. "Sister, this is my brother, Douglas Potter." The two shook hands.

"Very nice meeting you," he said, withdrawing his hand a little too quickly.

"I understand you're from Los Angeles? This weather must be quite a contrast to what you're used to. I'm grateful you're here to support Elizabeth—I know she appreciates it." Sister Antoinette had a knack for sizing up people. Doug was a good administrator, but his impatience was insensitive to Elizabeth's emotional needs. He was eager to exit the polite conversation, but the nun was there to do the Lord's work and that was what mattered. Elizabeth's experience was one she needed, wanted, to learn more about. She turned to Elizabeth. "We'll talk again soon and make a date to finish that dream. God bless you and keep you, Elizabeth." The tone of her voice was profoundly reverent.

"I'll be in touch." Elizabeth said.

The nun sauntered toward the elevator bank. Sister Antoinette had the rare ability to manifest from thin air and disappear the same way.

"That was interesting. What's her attachment to you?" Doug asked.

"She likes me, what can I say?" but Elizabeth knew that wasn't the reason.

⁂

The therapist's office contained the stereotypical trappings—a leather couch, two high-backed easy chairs and a desk. There was not much to define the personality of the room, but the gray-green walls and a few certificates and non-descript commercial paintings. Elizabeth and the therapist, Peter Candless, sat in one of the two chairs positioned across from each other. He was a slight man, bearded, about fifty and wore a turtleneck that was frayed at the neck, jeans and a tweed jacket. He poised a lined yellow pad on the arm of the chair.

"Tell me why you think you're here, Elizabeth. Do you prefer Liz or?" the therapist asked.

"My brother and friends call me Liz. Stephen always said he liked my full name." An uncomfortable silence caused her to straighten her jacket and re-cross her legs before she spoke again. "I was unable to cope with anything after my husband's death. Every aspect of living overwhelmed me, and the pain was unbearable. It felt like I was in a black hole and all I could think was I wanted out, I didn't want to be here. There was nothing left without Stephen," she whispered, as she toyed with the tissue in her hands. "I wanted to be with him."

The words hung in the air for what seemed a longer time than was necessary. Peter made notes on his tablet and looked up at Elizabeth.

"I see. How are you feeling right now?" he pressed.

"Having my brother here has helped. We don't know each other very well, since he is older than I am. He was hardly ever home—he left for college when I was nine. We corresponded and talked a little and he was home for holidays, but we were never close due to our age difference. He's been fabulous, but I feel guilty that I've put him through this," Elizabeth said, more to the painting behind Peter's desk than to the therapist.

"Is it possible that your brother can be more involved in your life now?" Peter asked.

"We live on opposite coasts. He's the major principal in his law firm in L.A. and has offered to have me move in with him and his wife and children til I get stronger. Start a new life out there. It would feel awkward and I never liked California. It was always my dream to live on the East Coast and we, I mean I, have this house and . . ." she dabbed her eyes and cheeks, "It's complicated."

"If you've realized that dream, Elizabeth, perhaps it's time to create a new one?" the therapist both asked and stated.

"My friend Marni offered to bridge the time between and have me move in with her for a few weeks or however long it takes to make arrangements to go west."

"That sounds like a reasonable plan to make the transition," Peter said. "What's keeping you from making that decision?"

"I keep thinking I could go back to the architectural firm I was under contract with before this happened and take on a small project, but then I think about being here with the holidays coming and being in the house and its memories . . ." sobs erupted. "See, this is where I get confused and don't know what to do." She squeezed her eyes voiding them of tears and blew her nose in the shredded tissue. Peter offered her another from the box he had ready on his desk.

"I appreciate that you are working on different possibilities, Elizabeth. You apparently have given it some thought. My job is to help you gain clarity and keep you safe as you move forward toward healing and functioning. Keeping your options open sounds helpful so we can explore them together and figure it out. Are you willing to do that?"

Elizabeth nodded, sat up straighter and assessed this person sitting across from her. He was seriously clinical, but she was dealing with grief and sifting through her feelings so it was probably a good thing that he was.

At the end of the session, Peter went to his desk and consulted his calendar and jotted her next appointment on his business card. He handed it to her and Elizabeth stood as she popped it into her purse and walked to the door.

She reached for the handle.

"I'll see you next week. Thank you. Say, could you tell me if Sister Antoinette has offices here?"

Peter Candless' unreadable expression altered ever so slightly. Elizabeth caught the subtle shift in his demeanor.

"I believe she lives in the convent next to the founding church. How do you know her?"

"We have unfinished business," Elizabeth said.

Chapter Fourteen

Old and New Business

Standing in the well-lit corridor adjacent to the administrative offices, Elizabeth and Doug shuffled paperwork between them. Doug crammed the last of the papers into his leather folder with the gold foil initials "DEP" imprinted on it, and tucked it underneath his arm.

"Would you like to grab a bite?" Maybe a little on the healthier side? His smile was complicit.

"Actually, that sounds good, but I thought I might catch up with Sister Antoinette while we're here."

"We can come back, if you like. I'm yours while we get you situated."

"Sure, okay. I think she's strangely interested in me—maybe it was something I said?" Elizabeth cast a devilish look at her brother. "More likely it's my soul she's after." Her offbeat humor came straight from the gene pool and was very much like her brother's. Ultimately, everything springs from there.

The two exited through the sheets of glass opening upon their approach and strolled into a blindingly bright day.

❧ ❧ ❧

Seated at closely arranged tables that were brimming with people in a harried lunch rush, they waited for their order.

"This is quite a place. Is it always like this?" Doug asked.

"As long as I can remember. The last time I was here was with Stephen." Her eyes misted a little and she shook her head to loosen the thought of him.

Doug reached across the table and took her hand.

"There will always be reminders. He must have been a helleva guy. I regret not making an effort to know him. I promise I won't make that mistake again." Doug unconsciously smoothed the collar underneath his crew neck sweater as if to let the discomfort escape and stared into her eyes. "I realize how lucky I am to have you, Liz. I keep saying it, but . . ." It was Doug's turn to get a little misty.

A white-aproned waiter brought two bowls made of hollowed-out bread and two green salads. He lifted the carved bread lid and a whoosh of steam rose into the air. Doug scooped up a spoonful of creamy broccoli soup, blew on it and raised it toward Elizabeth. "Bon appétit!"

She mirrored the gesture back to him.

"I think this afternoon I'd like to get my office organized. That would really help. Marni did the best she could arranging the essentials to be paid and kept the wolves away from the door, but I need some hands-on time. I just haven't had the energy or interest.

"Sounds like a good place to start. I'll set up the hospital and medical files that you'll need for reference. That's a nightmare you don't need right now." Doug said between bites. "What is this really all about with you and Sister Antoinette?"

"I told you, when I was in the hospital I started to tell her about my dream or vision or whatever it was and she said she wanted to hear the end of it." Pointing to her head, "It's a little fuzzy, but I know it's rattling around in there. I'm sure it'll come back to me." She popped a half-moon-shaped cucumber into her mouth. "It's really more the feeling it left me with and the fact that my heart had stopped before I had the dream." She avoided eye contact with her practical brother. "I've heard about near-death-experiences and..."

"Sis, you can't believe in that stuff. It's just your brain firing neurons or who knows what." Doug pushed back from the table and tossed his napkin next to his bread bowl. "I thought you had more gray matter than that, Liz," Doug said as he reached for his water glass. He took a healthy drink and swallowed hard.

Elizabeth's eyes welled and she looked away from her brother. "I'm sure Antoinette would disagree with you."

The waiter appeared to remove their dishes. "Would you care to see the dessert tray? Our specials today are Blueberry Apple Crisp and Pumpkin Mousse."

☙ ☙ ☙

Elizabeth's home office was eclectic, designed to reflect her refined tastes combined with rustic charm. It was located off the entry and separated by mullioned glass French doors. Both she and Doug were sorting envelopes and papers and concentrating on making neat stacks. Elizabeth put sticky notes on top to identify each of the piles.

"It's incredible that Stephen had life insurance. Young couples don't usually take care of those kinds of things." Doug said.

"Stephen was a detail guy. Meticulous. Dotted all the i's and crossed all the t's. He would be horrified to see the way I've let things get in such a mess. Always the engineering mind—that's how he thought—everything in order and multiple systems in place."

"You can start fresh now." Doug checked the sticky notes on the piles. "Looks like things are pretty much together here." He got up and headed for the doors. "I need to get back to the caseloads I left dangling. My partners and staff have been phenomenal, but there's a limit."

"I understand, but I selfishly don't want you to go. You've made me feel like there's normalcy and hope, and a tomorrow with me in it. I owe you, Doug." Her sincerity was palpable.

☙ ☙ ☙

Admiring the neatness of a once disheveled room, Elizabeth picked up the handset and punched in Marni's number and reclined on the small floral settee in the cozy office. The voicemail picked up. "Hey, Marni. I'm feeling better, not super strong, but having Doug here is great. We've had good catch up time and he's added a lot of his perspective to things. If your offer still stands to put up with me for a few weeks, I'd love that. Call me when you can. Love ya."

Elizabeth ended the call and her mind drifted toward the ancient pair of figures from her dream who hovered at the edge of her awareness. She realized the encounter was a powerful experience which left her transformed in a way she could not explain, even to herself.

❧ ❧ ❧

Elizabeth busied herself getting the last of the dishes put away before her appointment at the hospital. Her sessions were going well, especially with Doug making arrangements to prolong his stay.

"I can drive, Doug. I have to sooner or later." Elizabeth tossed the strap of her sleek tan leather bag onto her shoulder. "I'll wade in the shallow end and work up to deep water. Maybe it will inspire me to who knows what?"

"I think I should go with you. If nothing else, for moral support?" Doug asked. "I can go shopping and pick up something for the kids and Jenna. Any good malls in the area?"

"More than you can handle," she smiled, as she cinched the belt of her off-white merino wool trench coat tight around her waist.

"I'm in. Let's go." Doug followed his sister out the front door into a day that was drippy and dark.

Chapter Fifteen

Days of Future Past

The Watchers never rested, as time was irrelevant in the cosmic continuum. Elizabeth's angels were no exception. Metatron swept into the crystalline room vibrating with violet light. He sat at a carved table stacked with ancient-looking tomes, his crimson robe draped over the padded bench. The atmosphere was imbued with a violet glow and his regal countenance matched the ambiance the room exuded. More a library, extensive shelves wrapped around corners and were filled with scrolls and parchment and tablets with curious marks on them. Leather-bound books were squeezed into every open space and niche within the room and the rooms beyond. Lamps aglow with violet light burned in the sconces on every wall illuminating the majestic figure as he contemplated which book to select from the pile on the table nearest his right elbow.

Thoughtfully, he chose a volume and carefully placed it in front of him. He closed his hooded lids over eyes that shone like obsidian marbles and breathed deeply; his exhale was a neon-blue vapor that was neutralized in the violet air. Opening his eyes, he let the pages fall open randomly. Metatron allowed his gaze to be magnetically drawn to a passage scrawled onto the brittle parchment and his eyes widened perceptibly. He traced his smooth shapely finger along the encryption and looked pleased, his expression laced with contentment.

The rooms began to fill with other angels who consulted the various documents just as Metatron had done, but he remained undistracted and absorbed the moment of revelation. He closed the book and rose and took it to a great long table on the perimeter of the room and placed it there. He patted the worn cover before he swept out of the room. The violet light clung to his deep red robes making them appear the richest royal purple. Metatron was a special archangel dedicated as the scribe of God to his cosmic duties that governed life and death—ones that he had performed since the beginning of consciousness on earth.

❧ ❧ ❧

Seeking a place to reflect upon his discovery, Metatron ambled into a field of brilliant emerald green grass. The light was vibrant and inviting and he appeared fluid and at one with the environment. Buoyed by his next assignment, he sought the solace of a glorious oak that had grown along the edge of the meadow. He nestled between two chunky roots that burrowed deep into the ground; its bark absorbed the warmth and emanated it against his back. Concentrating on the horizon, Metatron calculated how he would knit the threads of chance together and slipped his Merkabah cube from a panel in his robe and gazed at it on his open palm. The healing power of the cube allowed him to open the channels for Elizabeth to live out her life's purpose through events that would make that possible. She would have to stay on the path and consent to an unknown future and its possibilities. Ah, but there was that thing about free will. He knew that humans could not let go of that which no longer served them—old ideas, relationships, feelings and thus frequently blocked his work. But he knew that his ward was trying to move on no matter how helpless and hopeless she felt after the loss of her husband and entire way of life. He knew there was a spark ignited within her to propel her forward, in this he was confident, but it was up to her to choose.

Movement in the distance caught his attention. It was Sandalphon, his twin. As twins are known to do, he must have sensed his brother's thoughts. He smiled at the angelic being who came into focus and appeared before him.

"Lazing against a tree looks like a wonderful idea." Sandalphon gracefully swooped in and settled into a niche that cradled his long elegant back. "I see you have consulted your cube," pointing to Metatron's familiar tool of healing.

Metatron nods. "I saw what was written about Elizabeth's future," Metatron said. "The records are clear. Our opportunity to reveal the threads of her fate will manifest soon." Metatron smiled. "We will be ready for whatever direction she chooses. If we can get her past the first threshold, she will have eyes to see and her course will be forever changed."

Sandalphon smoothed his robes and let his eyes rest shut, as he basked in the goldenness of the day.

૪૯ ૪૯ ૪૯

Elizabeth sorted through the clothes in her closet deciding what she fit into and what she needed to donate. She had lost weight since Stephen's death and found little in her wardrobe that appealed to her tastes. She felt different, was different, and her clothes were a reflection of that other life she had. Yes, she would be starting back to work, but it was more than that. She pulled dresses, skirts, held them up and tossed in one pile or another on the bed. Her thoughts drifted toward the garments of the magnificent beings she had encountered—they were timeless in their elegance and classic beauty. That was what she was after. She wanted a new look because she felt different. She wondered why she would be thinking of them now. It had to be that deep burgundy color in the floral print blouse she tossed in a third pile of "maybes" that kindled the association. In any case, Elizabeth was surprised to be energized by thoughts of creating something new.

The winds rattled the panes of her bedroom windows and pulsed through the maples outside, stripping them of the last of their leaves. Thanksgiving approached and it was hard to believe winter, normally a time of hibernation and incubation, was close behind. Doug made arrangements to remain in New Bristol through the holidays and conduct work from there, thanks to tapping the latest technology, so her plans to move to Marni's never materialized. His extended stay was a bonus she had not counted on, and it turned out to be the brightest time she could remember since Stephen's passing. It was literally just what the doctor would have ordered.

She was excited that Jenna and the kids would be flying in for a few days and they would all be attending Marni's family's huge traditional Thanksgiving dinner. Marni was the youngest of nine children and with aunts, uncles, cousins, spouses and nieces and nephews who lived in the immediate area, Thanksgiving was a major undertaking. Elizabeth felt lucky to be invited and thought how Stephen would have loved it. She stopped her thoughts from going in that direction, and scooped up a pile of clothes in each arm off the bed and left the "maybe" pile behind. She went to the living room and placed one armful at a time into a box and flapped the cardboard over it. She swiveled and walked away, but returned and re-opened one of the flaps and combed through a couple of items on top, then rolled her eyes, tucked the flap back into the carton and walked away without looking back.

Chapter Sixteen

Revelations

Logan Airport was a beehive—or worse. Elizabeth could not recall a time before when it was this phrenetic. "I think I should drive around, and you go in and find them."

Elizabeth craned her neck to see if there was double or triple parking possible for her and Doug to switch out so she could drive. She pointed and said, "Up there by the bus kiosk. Pull behind the blue car while they're loading."

Doug edged up close to the man plunking luggage into the trunk of a vintage Lincoln Towne car and shoved it in park. Checking his cell for last minute updates, Doug snugged up his coat and collar and braced for the elements before he exited. "Their flight was only delayed by a little. I can't imagine where they are."

"There are so many people they may have taken the wrong concourse." Elizabeth opened her door and met him at the back of the car. "I'll keep circling. Watch for me as I may not be able to get over to the curb. It's really bitter out. Here, take my scarf in case someone needs it." Unwrapping a plush glen plaid from her neck, she shoved it into her brother's hands.

Doug waved holding up the scarf and disappeared into the buzzing mass of people.

❧ ❧ ❧

Elizabeth sped down the parkway toward New Bristol relieved to be untangled from the knots of traffic surrounding the terminal. Jenna was in the passenger seat, her long auburn hair pulled back to reveal her lightly freckled oval face. Her stature was petite, but was one who could hold her own making her the perfect match for Doug who sat between his two children in the back. Channing, an engaging eight-year-old, was wearing Aunt Liz's scarf.

"How much longer, Aunt Liz?" Channing was a smaller version of her mother, red-haired and spunky.

"We'll be there before you know it." Elizabeth smiled to herself. Her thoughts wandered toward the family she and Stephen might have had. "You're pretty quiet back there, Jackson." Elizabeth peeked into the rearview mirror to see a little sprite drowsing on his father's arm.

"We're all dealing with the time difference and they hardly slept last night," Jenna said.

"I slept!" Channing wasn't admitting to trip anxiety.

"We'll rest up as soon as we get to Aunt Liz's," Jenna said to her daughter, but looked toward her sister-in-law. "If this is too much for you, we can stay in a hotel. Really, we understand."

"Having you here is part of my therapy. I appreciate you sharing Doug with me for this long because I wouldn't have made it this far without him. Hope you'll enjoy an old-fashioned New England experience–this time of year is magical, or at least I think it is. But you may have culture shock coming from L.A. and . . ."

Jenna reached for Elizabeth's arm. "I'm looking forward to getting to know you. It's the way it should have been, before . . ."

"We all take things for granted until they're not there." Elizabeth squeezed her sister-in-law's hand. The two women made eye contact for the briefest instant, when a snore erupted from the backseat.

≈ ≈ ≈

By four o'clock it was nearly dark. Jenna stood at the mudroom door and motioned to her children who played in the back yard. Channing was at the back-fence line gathering a collection of brilliant orange and red maple leaves and Jackson bounced a ball against the side of the house. "Come on, you two."

Jenna ushered them in and told them to take off their coats and wash their hands directing them to the half-bath between the living room and Elizabeth's office. Elizabeth stood at the stove stirring a cast iron pot of navy bean soup. "They seem like really good kids."

"They are. We try to limit their time with the devices and I insist on outdoor time. You know how it is these days." Jenna said.

"I see so many kids glued to a screen. Seems like they miss a lot. Don't get me wrong, I do live in the real world, but playing outside is refreshing to see."

"We live in that real world, too, and it's a constant struggle that will probably get worse before it gets better. We try to set a good example, but . . ." Jenna patted her iPhone in the back pocket of her jeans. "Anything I can do to help?"

"Everything's done. Is it too early for a toast? Champagne or I have a Cabernet."

"I'm ready, even if it is only lunchtime in California!" Jenna answered.

※ ※ ※

After dinner and making short order of cleaning up the kitchen with two helpers, Elizabeth nested in the overstuffed chair and Doug and Jenna snuggled up on the couch. The small fireplace that Stephen had converted to a gas log flame provided just the right ambiance of light and warmth to create a cozy atmosphere. "You'll love Marni. She'll adopt you, I know she will."

"She must be special." Jenna said.

"One of a kind. Thank God for her." Doug said, directing a loving glance at his sister.

"Her family is even more amazing. How she keeps track of everyone is miraculous."

"You met her at your workplace? Right?" Jenna asked.

"We all need our angels and she was there from my first day making sure I knew all the ins and outs of the prevailing politico and water cooler gang." Elizabeth responded. "What about you, Jenna? After the kids are older, what are your plans for getting out of the house—or maybe not!"

"I've thought about it, maybe I'll try something new. Being a personal trainer or fitness guru in one's forties isn't exactly in high demand, especially in Southern Cal. We'll see. I wish I had talent for art like you do, Liz. Your renderings are amazing—almost like photographs, but with more character and nuances."

"You've always said you wanted to go back to school and maybe get into a health care field." Doug chimed in.

"God knows there's a need, Jenna. I could see you doing physical therapy or maybe . . ." Elizabeth yawned. "'Scuse me. Think it's time to call it a night. Do you mind? She got out of her chair and stretched her arms over her head then picked up her half-filled goblet. "If you two want to stay up, you know where everything is." Elizabeth hugged them both and retreated toward the back of the house leaving Doug and Jenna looking perplexed at her abrupt departure.

෴ ෴ ෴

Lingering with the last of her cabernet, she burrowed underneath the covers pulling the down comforter to her chin. Elizabeth snuggled into the welcome warmth of her bed. There was not a night that went by when she did not miss Stephen, but after his death, she got rid of their old mattress and ordered a new one that now held only her scent. She found the toggle on her earphones and adjusted the volume. Her therapist suggested classical music to help with sleep since Elizabeth's sleep medications were tightly controlled. Beethoven's Moonlight Sonata was a favorite on her playlist that lifted her to another dimension, so she put it on repeat.

Elizabeth's thoughts traveled from one topic to the next creating threads that crossed and tangled. She suspected her niece and nephew were instructed to be on their best behavior because Aunt Liz had been ill and wondered if Channing and Jackson would be the only children in her life. She recognized those thoughts were circular, and as Peter pointed out, did not move her forward. Or did they? Jenna was a beautiful grounding rod for Doug amid the trappings of success. And my brother—what an unexpected gift. Amazing what maturity does for people and in the end family is everything.

She reached for her wine and focused on the deep red color that lulled her into that nether land where consciousness surrenders. She put the glass on the nightstand and drifted off easily. Her musings led her into a deep sleep where she experienced dream after dream. At 3:18 a.m., the digital clock numerals glowed green in the darkness and Elizabeth was catapulted awake, her body a tuning fork. She shot straight up causing the covers to fall away and she gasped taking in a full breath, heart pounding. She waited until she oriented herself, took note of the time and waited for her heart to slow down to a regular rhythm before she lay back down.

The dream was real. Metatron and Sandalphon met her in the red realm and escorted her to the other realms that existed beyond the horizon. She had been there before, but it looked different this time. The land of blue, a land of cleansing and preparation and peace. The sky was a sheet of endless blue, a vivid backdrop against the sapphire palace that gleamed its welcome to Elizabeth. She was stunned at its elegance and grandeur. Blue hydrangeas and forget-me-nots dotted the landscape and a carpet of tiny lobelia covered the ground surrounding the azurite slabs that configured the footpath to the palace. Blue had an immediate calming effect and with each step, she felt more at peace.

The twin angels held the double doors open and she entered. Sapphire chandeliers sparkled with blue light and the benches and chairs were encrusted with blue topaz stones. A guest book with blue crystals lay open and shimmered on the parson's table. Metatron swept past her and offered her a billowy blue plume inviting her to write in the book. She accepted the feather and wrote her name among hundreds, probably thousands, that had been recorded before her. A spiral staircase constructed of cobalt blue stained glass was off to the right, and Sandalphon floated upward until he disappeared, then Metatron followed. Dare she float up as well? She took a step, and another, then lifted off her feet and ascended the stairs with barely a footfall.

The landing was a flood of blue light and the vistas from its long narrow windows revealed a sea of blue meadows and lakes and infinite sky. Elizabeth was drawn into the backdrop of this pristine beauty and a sense of calm permeated every part of her. She thought this might be heaven, but it also felt like it would lead to something more. She watched her guides float down a maze of corridors, the turquoise walls inviting her to follow. Catching up, she followed them to a room where all three entered.

Elizabeth could hardly absorb the beauty. Pale blue velveteen lined the walls to the top of the clerestory. Shafts of light that matched the hue of the fabric streamed in to highlight the shimmering richness. There was one round table in the center of the room that was inlaid with glistening blue jewels. On top of the table was the dusty tome that Metatron had viewed in the record room; he stood with his hand on it awaiting her attention. Elizabeth thought the book looked odd among such opulence never dreaming that it was the most precious and valuable thing in the palace of the blue band.

Sandalphon hovered beside Elizabeth, his height dwarfing her. Or was it his presence that loomed large? Probably both. Metatron traced his finger along a passage and read to Elizabeth. She heard what he said, but it slipped through her mind the instant she heard it. She imagined it recorded somewhere in her psyche to be retrieved later when she was ready to hear it.

She opened her eyes to white sunlight streaming through the blinds in her room. The next thing she heard was Jackson running down the hall. "Auntie Liz! Time to get up!"

Chapter Seventeen

Thanksgiving

The Petrakis clan was a loving and cantankerous mixture of old world and new. The matriarchs schlepped food from the adjacent kitchen to a twelve-foot table that was set up buffet style. Kids' card tables were stationed in the family room and on the screened back porch where a space heater took off the late autumn chill. Elizabeth and Marni hung out in the kitchen taking directions from the elder women.

Demetra Petrakis wiped her forehead with her apron. "Marni, can you and your friend check on the silverware and napkins? I don't think there's enough out there. Mama Petrakis brought two or three sets. They're on the floor in the pantry."

"Sure thing, Mom. Anything else?" Marni's springy black curls bounced on her shoulders, as she bolted through the old-fashioned swinging door to the dining room to check the sideboard set up with condiments and table settings.

After a brief assessment, Marni swung back through the kitchen. "I'll add more in case," she said to her mom who was in the process of making a vat of gravy.

Elizabeth followed her friend trying to be helpful. "Hand them to me, Marn..."

The young women buzzed around the others until Demetra shooed them out. "Go enjoy yourselves—we'll eat pretty soon." Several turkeys and hams rested on carving boards and the scent was intoxicating.

Doug and Jenna mixed easily with the crowd engaging young couples in animated conversation. Doug caught Jackson running a couple of times and the last time Doug gave him a time out, but Jackson didn't care as there was so much going on. Egg nog, spiced punch, apple cider and wine flowed and the mood of the day was elevated by the time they were ready to eat.

Nicholas Petrakis stood at the head of the table and clinked a fork against a crystal goblet several times in order to get everyone's attention. Eventually, the din died down and even the kids were shushed into being quiet. "Mama Petrakis says everything's ready to eat so let us join in a prayer and blessing." People stood around the table and held hands and bowed their heads. "Thank you, God, for the bounty we are about to receive today and for the love and blessings of our homes and families. For our new friends and old and for providing for us in our lives. Amen." Nichols held Demetra's hand and he raised them into the air.

❧ ❧ ❧

After too many slices of pumpkin pie, the men lazed on couches and chairs, watched football and snoozed. Marni, Jenna and Elizabeth were busy sorting out clean dishes and making stacks on the counter of those that did not belong in the Petrakis kitchen. A tall lean Norwegian-looking man crept through the door and tiptoed up behind Marni and put his finger to his lips to indicate, "quiet."

"Want some coffee before you go?" Marni offered turning around with the pot in her hand. "Oh, my God! What are you doing, Josh?" The lanky man pressed Marni's ample body to him in a deep embrace, giving her a kiss.

"There's more to life than dishes. Time to stop." Marni set the coffee pot on the counter and the two turned and left the room, but not before Marni shot a wink at her friend.

"How long have those two been together?" Jenna asked folding up a dish towel and picking up the pot.

"About two years . . . seems serious, but you never know with Marni." Elizabeth replied.

The women exited the kitchen with their cups in hand and found Jackson and Channing on the living room floor playing games on tablets and Doug snoring with the men on the couch. "He may never recover," Jenna said, as she wafted the coffee under his nose and teased him awake. "Hey, you."

Doug stirred and stretched. "Okay, okay," he said, and checked his watch.

※ ※ ※

After thank-yous, hugs, and well wishes for the upcoming holidays, the Potter clan piled into the Mercedes. Doug started to back out of the driveway when a black SUV appeared from nowhere on his right. The driver honked his horn and Doug hit the brakes bouncing everyone forward in the car.

"Doug, watch where you're going," Jenna scolded. Elizabeth observed the vehicle nearly plow into her side door and turned to glare at the driver of the car. She vaguely remembered seeing him during the course of the day, a friend of Marni's cousin or something, but this time, their eyes connected.

"You okay back there?" Doug asked his passengers.

The faintest smile crossed Elizabeth's lips.

Chapter Eighteen

Opening Doors

The office building was ultra-modern industrial, the ideal venue for an architectural firm. The multi-storied edifice was glass and wood, but inside the polished cement floors made the lobby echo-y. Elizabeth's soft-soled boots made a soft squeaky sound, as she approached the reception desk fashioned out of a thick chunk of etched glass. The young East Indian woman seated behind it had enormous soulful eyes that danced when she looked up to see Elizabeth. She skirted around the desk.

"Chandra!" Elizabeth opened her arms and swallowed up her friend's petite frame.

"Elizabeth," Chandra said, stepping back to assess her. "You look well. Are you back to work now?"

"Just starting out small, but I'll be around—I'm trying it out to see how it goes." Elizabeth responded.

The phone on the desk lit up and Chandra squeezed Elizabeth's hand before returning to answer it through her headset. Elizabeth waved good-bye and pointed at her watch then headed for the elevators.

๛ ๛ ๛

Fred Oliphant, Operations Director, had his door closed. His etched stainless-steel nameplate was hard to read in the subdued lighting, but Elizabeth could find his office by rote. She knocked and the door gave way and she peeked in.

"Fred?" she inquired.

The middle-aged man popped up from behind his desk. "Dropped my goddam pen again," he dusted off his pants at the knees. "Elizabeth. Come in, sit down. Glad you decided to harass us again." His hard edges were not typical of the creative types.

"Fred. Thanks for your patience and having me back. I'm grateful for all you and the staff did for me while I was, uh, away," Elizabeth said.

There was an awkward silence, but Fred spoke up after scrutinizing her with laser precision. "You okay now?"

Elizabeth nodded, but wanted to get down to business to avoid personal questions. "Anything new I need to be brought up to speed on with the Bauer account?"

"Grant Bauer has decided to scale down the size of his building and new renderings will be needed. Since you have the preliminary concepts on the bigger project, how soon do you think you could get them to me?" Fred was always direct and more sensitive than people gave him credit for and she liked that about him.

"I'll see Greta on my way out and have her send the updated files. Maybe two weeks?" Elizabeth ventured a guess. "I'll be more specific after I get a look at the changes."

"Not too much pressure?" Fred cast a probing eye in her direction. "He's ready to commit on this one."

"For you, I move mountains." Elizabeth joked.

୬୬ ୬୬ ୬୬

Christmas music wafted through the air in Elizabeth's home office, as she worked at her computer assembling the data that would produce the renderings needed for the Bauer project. It gobbled up her day and Doug found her absorbed in her work when he peered through the glass doors of her office.

"You need a break. It's a good practice. I force myself to walk away from the grind and I'm never sorry. How about a short walk?" Doug swung open one of the doors.

"I'm seriously at a crucial point. Give me another half hour."

"It'll be nearly dark then." Doug's eyes were pleading.

"Five minutes," she relented. Elizabeth enjoyed having male energy around the house and she wondered how she would cope after he left. She hadn't realized her need for companionship was as deep as it was. No wonder she languished.

Doug held up his hand with fingers splayed. "Five minutes."

※ ※ ※

The leaves were long gone and lawns were dried up and brown. The wind was icier, but the sun was out, albeit a low winter sun that radiated little warmth. Doug and Elizabeth speed walked to get their circulation going, but eventually became competitive and a race down the sidewalks of New Bristol's quaint neighborhoods ensued.

Red-cheeked and nearly out of breath, the siblings finally stopped and cut across the street to an empty small park and playground. They jumped on the merry-go-round and started to spin.

"Let's call it a draw?" Doug suggested.

"If you say so, big brother," Elizabeth agreed. "You're right. I do feel better. How do you know these things? When did you get to be so smart?"

"Operating my own business, a wife, two kids and PTA meetings opens one up to a whole world of wisdom," Doug answered, then realized it might have sounded insensitive.

"I get it—it's just not happened for me yet." She dragged her feet in the dry dirt beneath the wheel that was still moving. "I wonder if it ever will," Elizabeth was wistful. "That's why you're here—to inspire and keep me looking forward to the possibilities, right?" A genuine smile conveyed a growing appreciation for her brother.

"Race you home!" Doug got up popping off the equipment onto the ground to a head start.

"There're sandwich fixings in the fridge. Let me finish up in my office and we'll throw something together," Elizabeth said, finding a hook in the entry for her coat.

Doug drew his cell out of his pocket and walked toward the kitchen. "I need to call Jenna and the kids before they go to bed and see if they're getting excited about their first New England Christmas."

Chapter Nineteen

Unfinished Business

Remnants of snow dotted the curbs and around bushes and the monochromatic dark gray sky promised more. Elizabeth was energized by the smell of snow in the air thinking New Bristol may indeed deliver a white Christmas to her West Coast family.

She walked from the hospital campus after her therapy session toward the founding church's steeple which was a prominent landmark not easy to miss. She was surprised Sister Antoinette had not suggested they meet at the hospital, but either way she wanted to satisfy her obligation before the holidays. It was characteristic of Elizabeth to keep her word. She was coming to terms with the desperation and anxiety of the past and was moving on without Stephen. Her therapy session went well with Peter and she felt strong and confident enough to face the vague discomfort that accompanied her encounters with Sister Antoinette.

The convent was part of the church grounds and was close to the same vintage as the church. Archways on the porch entrance departed from the linear design of the church, but they were perfectly suited to house the clergy dedicated to the service of humankind. She ambled up the path and thought it odd that tangled remains of dead annuals were still in the concrete pots on the porch, as she pulled the massive wood door toward her and stepped into the warmth of an inviting sitting room. She did not expect to see the formality of a front desk when a nun appeared from behind a stack of cabinets. She indicated Elizabeth could call Sister Antoinette on the house phone and pointed to it and a directory list in a plastic sleeve taped on the desk. Hallways on either side led to rooms where the sisters lived and an atrium in the center of the core space provided light and a lovely organic ambiance.

Elizabeth waited in one of the overstuffed brocade chairs; she removed her soft knit hat and gloves and pulled from her purse a small package of notecards printed with her hand-crafted renderings of historical buildings. Sister Antoinette appeared in front of her almost as soon as Elizabeth heard the now familiar sound of her garments that rustled when she walked. She stood and smiled. "Sister Antoinette."

"There is a small meditation and prayer room where we can have some privacy. Being home agrees with you—you look wonderful." The nun pivoted and headed down the north arm of the hallway with Elizabeth in tow. She followed her into a wood-paneled room with a prie-dieu, two benches and side chairs. Paintings of Jesus and Mother Mary and plaster crucifixes were mounted on every wall with a heavy swag across the top of a small stained-glass window. The smoky scent of candles and subdued light created an "otherworld" atmosphere.

Sitting across from each other, Elizabeth handed the nun the small package to break the ice.

"How kind of you, dear." Antoinette pulled off the green satin bow and examined the notes.

"These are prints from my early work—I thought you might like to have them." Elizabeth offered.

"They are lovely. Your talent is apparent. Thank you." She laid them on a side table and fastened her attention on Elizabeth. "I thought this room might be a bit more, uh, personal away from the clinical setting. And you are obviously doing well?"

"My brother has been a gift. I never dreamed I could be so fortunate to have the support he's given. My therapy is winding down, I think, at least I feel a lot stronger, clearer. . ." Elizabeth wanted to continue about her personal life, but that was not what the nun was waiting to hear.

"In your message you said you recalled more of your experience, or dream as you call it?" The nun lasered in on Elizabeth. "I appreciate that you are willing to tell the rest of it. I have an interest and believe that it is somehow key to your complete healing." The nun fixed her gaze above Elizabeth's head on a painting that depicted Mary draped in a blue mantle holding her infant son.

"I'm frankly wondering why you are so curious about it. I never seem to get far enough into the vision to get to the end. Maybe if I concentrate harder, I'll be able to tell you more and satisfy your curiosity and mine. Perhaps it is no more complicated than we have something in common with the loss of our mothers at an early age."

Antoinette smiled thinly and Elizabeth responded in kind, because she was reminded that it represented another loss in her life and a new sense of compassion stirred for the nun.

"I'm sure it was hard for you." Elizabeth said softly.

"The void was filled with faith and my calling to spiritual service." Antoinette shut down the conversation. Her ability to receive empathy was difficult.

"I'll need to start at the beginning and work into it. When I reflect on the overall memory it's initially peaceful, but is like a dream where you can't grasp the ending, and no matter how hard you try, it eludes you." Elizabeth re-positioned herself in her chair and drew in a few deep breaths. She knew to concentrate on the color red that triggered re-entry into the dream and searched her surroundings to find it. The only red she saw was the blood that streamed down the face of a tortured Jesus, a result of the crown of thorns savagely pressed on his head. She forced herself to keep her eyes fastened on the crimson drops, and swiftly entered the realm.

Elizabeth eased into a light trance. Sister Antoinette squinted and inched closer to the young woman with every change in voice and eye movement. Antoinette was attentive to each word and nuance of the experience. She leaned in as Elizabeth recounted the red, orange, yellow, green and blue realms, repeating the same details of their magical beauty as before.

Elizabeth paused and partially opened her eyes. Her face softened when she saw Metatron and Sandalphon manifest in the room and seamlessly usher her into the indigo realm. Once there, Elizabeth remembered.

"The night was inky black and royal blue with millions of sparkling diamonds overhead. The dazzling brilliance lured me off the sapphire-paved path toward a dark tunnel where Metatron and Sandalphon loomed as sentries at the entrance of a cave. They were swathed in a shimmering indigo aura that flowed in sync with their movements, as they propelled themselves through the opening. I followed them deep into a cavern alive with glistening crystals that were a blue so deep they were almost black.

"Awed by the mysterious surroundings, the archangels conveyed that the kingdom of the indigo band would prepare me for the violet realm which was sacred to all who entered. I was told that in the indigo vibration I would be able to experience the gap between the infinite and finite and possess the ability to cross between them. Beyond where we lingered I saw a majestic bridge that spanned a vast pool of dark water. They effortlessly swept across the bridge, but I was reluctant to follow them. I feared I may not be able to return, but they assured me it would be my choice to return—or not. Polished blue-black slabs covered the surface of the bridge and were magnetically charged. When I stepped on the threshold of the bridge, a jolt of cosmic energy expanded in my body. I continued across and looked up into the inky vastness above and let myself be swallowed up in its depth and mystery. Before I knew it, I had traversed the dark channel of water and reached my companions who waited for me on the other side."

Antoinette's breathing was shallow and sweat dotted her forehead and nose. She removed her glasses and repositioned herself, as if eager for the next words, alternating her gaze between Elizabeth and the image of Mother Mary.

"I was aware of hands on my head and I recognized a softness to the air and that I was in a different realm. It was pure violet—a vibrant royal purple that was woven into every space of this kingdom. A palace glowed as a solitary amethyst jewel and emanated a powerful energy that made me lightheaded."

"'You have been prepared successfully for the next level of your journey, Elizabeth. You have experienced a change in consciousness. The entire body of your life events are registered as stepping stones that have delivered you to this moment of transformation.' Metatron's velvety voice was soothing and it settled me. 'We have seen what is written in the Book of Life and you are close to completing the restoration needed to continue the evolution of your existence. Although an infinite palette of choices has always been available, you have aligned with those that were for your highest good, although it was not always apparent.' Both angels looked to the heavens and their presences cocooned me in peace."

Antoinette could hardly breathe. Her suspicions were validated. These were the angels of legend documented in the forbidden blasphemous records and Elizabeth's experience gave credence to the fact they existed. How else could Elizabeth, a non-Catholic, know of them unless her vision was real? Antoinette knew her medical files stated that she was declared legally dead, but was revived after heroic medical intervention—or was it Elizabeth's choosing? With the nun's long tenure as a spiritual counselor, she had heard similar stories from those who had returned from death's doors with the mercy of the good Lord. But she had never encountered one who had confirmed the existence of the Grigori, The Watchers, and it was a personal coups that exceeded all proportions. She was pleased with herself, yet somewhat afraid, as it released a genie from a forbidden bottle.

Elizabeth stirred, opened her eyes and was fully awake. She focused on the crucifix on Antoinette's chest and realized it was mirrored in the sculpture of the suffering of Christ on the wall behind her. She clutched her stomach feeling slightly nauseous in the closeness of the room. As she sat up straighter and forced her awareness into the present moment, she noted the perspiration and wide eyes on the nun's face. "I don't think that was all of it, but all I could recall."

"You had a remarkable experience, Elizabeth, but your vision was different from the accounts of others who have shared a similar journey. The one about that place we visit between life and death." Antoinette wiped her face with a tissue stored in her sleeve and adjusted her glasses, as she stood and brushed down her skirts.

"I should be going." Elizabeth was grateful to stand, but needed to steady herself.

"Perhaps we can meet another time. I am available if you, uh, remember more details. Antoinette's gaze penetrated as Elizabeth reached for the handle of the prayer room door and opened it. "You are indeed a light that shines a little brighter." Antoinette patted Elizabeth's shoulder.

"Merry Christmas, Sister."

Elizabeth waved good-bye and left Antoinette standing in the chapel doorway.

Chapter Twenty

Threshold

Delicious aromas of a hearty stew and bread baking filled Elizabeth's bungalow with an invitation of warmth and nourishment for the body and soul. A bare noble fir Christmas tree stood in the front window of Elizabeth's living room. It replaced the couch that she put with its mate on the opposite side of the room to form an "L" shape. Elizabeth studied the arrangement and thought she liked how it looked and might keep it that way after the tree was removed. Jenna and the kids would be arriving shortly and they could decorate the tree after dinner. She bought new ornaments because the memories attached to the old ones in boxes in the attic were too emotionally charged.

The silver Mercedes pulled into the driveway and emptied Jenna, the kids and Doug onto her front porch. Seeing their arms loaded with luggage and boxes and holiday bags, Elizabeth ran to the door to welcome them inside.

"Hey, guys! The first Christmas miracle—you made your flights! Amazing for this time of year, but then, sadly, the weather's cooperated." Elizabeth gestured toward the cloudless sky before she shut the door. Channing nuzzled up to her aunt and hugged her hard, but Jackson ran for the tree and ornament boxes. Doug and Jenna joined in the hug.

"Feels like we're coming back home. The kids can hardly wait to share at school how they celebrated Christmas in New England with their Aunt Liz," Jenna said. "Can we put some of this under the tree?"

"Sure, and after supper, we can decorate it, if you're up for it," Elizabeth said to Jenna and her nephew who was investigating the tree from top to bottom.

"Cool!" Jackson grinned.

"What smells so good?" Doug asked. "Whatever it is, I want some."

☙ ☙ ☙

"I can't believe we don't have snow, but you never know." Elizabeth was cross-legged on the floor opening boxes of ornaments and fastening hooks into the metal hoops on the bulbs before handing to one of the children. "It probably feels like winter considering the temps in California. What was it, Jen, about eighty when you left today?" Doug and Jen snuggled on the couch watching the tree come to life with its colorful decorations.

"Looking good, guys, but I think you missed a spot in front of the window. We want it to be pretty from the outside, too." Liz said, as she uncoiled her legs and pushed up into a standing position with ease. "Anyone want more hot chocolate?"

The kids chimed, "Me," in unison.

"I'll help you. Doug can supervise out here." Jenna offered.

Elizabeth stirred the pan of chocolate meditatively. "I've been doing a lot of thinking, Jen, and it makes sense for me to go to L.A.—take a break, mix things up. I know you're worried I may slip back into depression and self-destruction trap, but I've learned a lot about normal emotions and I'm discovering tools that help like visualization and keeping a "positive" diary where I only list all the good stuff that happens during the day, but I know it will feel like a tomb in here after the holidays. Oh, sorry, didn't mean to, well, I thought I could lease this place for a year or maybe list it and see what happens. Offer still good?"

Jenna brightened. "Are you kidding? Have you told Doug? Our household is pretty chaotic most of the time with the kids' activities and mine, but I would love to introduce you around." Jenna held the mugs while Elizabeth poured.

"It wouldn't be for several months, but it would be a goal as long as you could be flexible." Elizabeth said, as she plopped a handful of puffy marshmallows on the top of each cup. "Let me surprise Doug."

"You'll make his Christmas. We want the best for you, Liz. Any way you can work it out. It would be a good time to catch up on missed opportunities to know each other better."

The two women trailed out of the kitchen to the living room where the tree decorating was nearly a fait accompli. "Good job!" Jenna said to her children. "Looks beautiful!"

Jackson ran for the hot chocolate and Channing fussed with a ball making it hang just right. "Thanks, mom."

"All due to my expert supervision," Doug smiled and picked up a frothy white angel tree-topper and held it out to the kids. "Who wants to put the angel on top?" Jackson beat his sister to his dad's side to stake his claim.

"Okay, sport." Doug passed the angel to his son and hoisted him up toward the top of the tree.

"Okay, Dad. She's on there!" Jackson said, and Doug lowered him to his feet.

"Let's fire up the lights!" Liz said, as she plugged in the brand new string of white twinkle lights. The tree glowed in the darkened room and Liz snapped a picture with her phone.

"Everyone stand in front of the tree . . . a little closer to get you all in." Liz snapped a couple of shots and then they all took turns posing to record the moment.

※ ※ ※

After settling the kids down in their respective beds, Jenna returned to the couch in living room and sat next to her husband. "Have you shared your news?" directing her question to Liz.

"I was waiting for you." Elizabeth said, then turned to Doug. "I told Jenna I'd like to take you up on your offer after the first of the year. There'd be a lot to do between now and then here, but it would give me something to look forward to . . . to move in another direction."

Doug grinned and leaned forward, elbows on knees. "Fantastic, Liz! You're in a different place in life now. I'd wager good bucks your experience of the big bad city won't be the same as you remember it. Don't get me wrong, I envy your lifestyle here, but the opportunities and potential . . ." He winked at Elizabeth. "You never know what might be waiting around the corner." Doug raised his mug in her direction. "To Liz and new beginnings," and downed the last of his cocoa.

The rhythm of blinking lights strung across the branches of the tree created a festive holiday glow. The house was blessedly quiet and Liz cozied herself in a comforter in her favorite chair reflecting on her decisions, her new-found family and how it all made the world bearable in just a few short months. She questioned everything including her decision to consider moving. She could not entirely trust her judgment with all she had been through, and it would take time to recover her confidence and sense of self, but within her a seed was germinating and a new Elizabeth Welles was emerging.

Wrapped in the fluffy comfort of her blanket, Elizabeth stared at the tree and her eyes fell on a large shiny red ball with swirly patterns of glitter that hung next to a blinking light. Its shimmer captured Elizabeth's attention and she was magnetized into the mystical promise of the red gateway to the world where the archangels dwelled. The portal opened and she followed the familiar paths and entered the rainbow color chambers that beckoned. She was driven homeward with invisible threads and Metatron and Sandalphon swiftly lead her to the threshold of the violet realm.

Chapter Twenty-One

White Light

Metatron as God's scribe sat at an exquisitely carved table with his ethereal hand resting on a magnificent tome of tooled leather and gilded pages. Sandalphon swirled his billowy robes around the corner brushing the library walls. Elizabeth followed him, eyes wide, as she took in the enormous walls filled with books and scrolls bathed in lavender light. The scenario was familiar, like déjà vu. That was it. She had no memory of her first visit to the violet realm, but of the time her consciousness was transformed at depth during the recounting of the indigo level to Sister Antoinette. The archangels told her of the white light and they have transported her to the realm in order to have her experience it again. Metatron ceremoniously opened the book and pointed a sculpted finger at her name and she tried to read the embellished Uncial script. She saw words on the page, but could not understand anything but her name. The white-haired angel impressed on her mind to try harder to read what was written. Elizabeth struggled to adjust her eyes to the dim violet light and attempted to read again, and this time she slowly made sense of the words as they came into focus. They outlined the milestones, the choices and events in her life and how her decisions created all that she had and ever would experience. The text explained that the possibilities were infinite, flexible and mutable with the exception of when we appeared on Earth and when we left; those were "written."

The information overwhelmed her and she faltered. Metatron gently caught her and lifted her upright, as if she was a feather. He closed the book with a "poof" then steered her toward an arched doorway that led to a round-shaped room where a circle inlaid with amethysts was incised on the floor. Her eyes lingered on the glistening jewels before her gaze was drawn upward where she observed a clear violet sky through an open oculus which reminded her of the Roman Pantheon. The flicker of a luminous violet flame suspended above the center of the circle caught her attention. Its light vibrated at a high frequency and she tingled as each cell in her body was awakened and opened her to an acute awareness. Metatron located himself on her right, Sandalphon on her left, the angels standing across from each other. There were several doors in the chamber and she focused on the one that was positioned directly across from her.

After basking in the violet light energy, each angel took one of Elizabeth's hands. They raised her above the ground and suspended her in the air, as they gently passed her through the flame. When Elizabeth reached the other side of the circle, the angels set her on the ground and unclasped her hands from theirs. She felt lighter, cleansed, and possessed a mental clarity unlike anything she had ever known before. She examined her body, her arms, hands and legs and saw that they possessed a faint violet aura. Before she could look to her angel companions for answers to the questions swirling in her mind, the door she had been attracted to opened noiselessly. Immediately, a radiant white light poured through its portals and filled the room. She looked around at Metatron and he nodded toward the door. She understood he wanted her to cross the threshold into the brilliant light.

With amazing ease, Elizabeth glided toward the light and entered into its radiance. The light created a cocoon of unconditional love enveloping her in an auric egg. Her guides remained in the circular room, but issued direction and information through what she had come to learn as the process of thought transmission. She received information that she was prepared to enter the light after the purification, while still in possession of free will.

She watched as the light transformed into a tunnel-shaped cone. In the distance where the light tapered, a figure began to emerge. The whiteness dazzled her senses and caused her heart to race. The figure slowly approached, moved closer, the outline of a man, someone familiar. She felt the pressure of white energy, as it rotated and pressed upon her flesh. She was stunned. He opened his arms to her and before her stood her beloved Stephen. Elizabeth's mind was afire with thoughts and memories and raw emotions of the last few months and she attempted to sort them out, but all she could focus on was the presence of her husband. Then she remembered, remembered how they met like this shortly after her own near-death. She fell into his embrace and they were entwined as one, savoring the reunion that she never thought she would experience again. It was a gift of priceless value. Elizabeth melted into the comfort and energy of her husband, grateful to have this second chance to be with him. No words were spoken, but he communicated, as he did before, that she had a life purpose to fulfill and must return to her world and dimension. Looking into her eyes, Stephen assured her he would always love her, but she must let him go so they could each fulfill their destinies in peace. Elizabeth could not release him and clung to stay in the space of their love throughout eternity. She felt him pull away and Stephen's image dissolved into the light. She grasped at his transparent form and reluctantly allowed herself to be drawn from his presence and pulled back through the door, as she watched him disappear into the glorious white light at the end of the tunnel.

The gentle caring hands of her guides, like midwives, supported her backward into the realm of consciousness jolting her awake. She slowly oriented herself to the familiar surroundings in her living room. The Christmas tree wrapped in its sparkly glow stood sentry in the window and reminded her that it was a symbol of hope and celebrated new birth and new way of life. She gave herself permission to revisit the feeling of Stephen holding her, basking in his closeness, his smell, his energy. But her reverie was interrupted by Jenna tiptoeing down the hallway to check on the children, which anchored her into reality.

Chapter Twenty-Two

Light Dawns

The perfume counters teemed with demonstrators who pressured the approaching holiday shoppers to lend their wrists and necks to be misted with samples of scents that eventually blended into one another. Marni enjoyed the attention while Elizabeth skirted the main cosmetic area and gestured to her friend that she would be in the shoe department.

Something sparkly and strappy had caught her eye and a new pair of shoes would be just the thing to dress up her faithful white party dress. As Marni continued to be drawn in to the cosmetic samples that were being liberally distributed, Elizabeth tagged onto a twenty-something young man who looked like he knew his fashion. She showed him the shoe and told him her size and he disappeared into a back room. In a flash, he returned with the box, extracted the shoes and neatly slipped them onto her feet. Elizabeth walked across the floor and smiled at the image of her shapely legs and slender foot wrapped in red satin and rhinestones in the slanted shoe mirror.

Marni found her posing her feet in all directions and trundled toward her laden with a variety of plastic bags. "Wow, Miz Liz, stunning! Look at you!"

Elizabeth beamed back at her.

"I think they're me," she giggled, not knowing what had come over her.

Marni commented that she liked Elizabeth's new attitude and that whatever was going on to keep it up. She noticed her friend's demeanor was lighter and freer and she was more like the old Liz before Stephen died.

Elizabeth held back sharing about her encounter with Stephen in the white light and that the experience was the cause for the shift, because Marni always shut her down when it came to anything spiritual or not of this world. Elizabeth longed to tell her how she knew now that we do not die, and our loved ones will be there for us. It was a new belief system which transformed her entire outlook on life. Only now did she realize that she had a second chance at it. She resolved to pinpoint the right timing to explain to Marni about the extraordinary series of events that surrounded her brush with death—to relate the whole story of the world of The Watchers and being in Stephen's arms again.

"They're not Jimmy Choos, but they'll do." She sauntered back to Marni, sat down and slipped off the shoes and placed them into the box. "Sold," she said, pulling on her soft boots, as Marni gave a thumb's up in warm approval.

After she paid for the shoes, Elizabeth returned to her friend who stayed seated in a long row of chairs among a sea of women trying on shoes. She interrupted Marni's focus on her phone. "Where to? Whose name did you draw this year?" Elizabeth asked. "With nine kids in the family, it seems like a sensible plan for the Petrakis."

"Brother Nick. He's easy. Anything to do with fishing has his name on it. I'll check out the sporting goods store and see what I can find." Marni slid her phone into her purse. "What are you getting Channing and Jackson for Christmas?" Marni asked.

Elizabeth shrugged. "Any suggestions? You know more about what kids their age want than I do."

"I'm up for hitting the toy store, but I'm dying for caffeine." Marni said.

Elizabeth pulled her friend up by the hand from the bank of chairs and they melded into the crowd of holiday shoppers.

૱ ૱ ૱

The malls were jammed with cars and people and nailing a parking space took longer than usual. With no snowfall since the first one of the season several weeks ago, most northeasterners did not complain and were out in force taking advantage of the clear streets. But Elizabeth was disappointed the snow never manifested the day she met with Antoinette. She knew Doug and Jenna would love the novelty of it and would fit into the Currier and Ives stereotype they probably harbored of New England.

The two women hiked into the cluster of stores and found a coffee bar where they squeezed onto a couple of stools at a high counter. Marni raised her hand to get the barista's attention and looked at her friend with an uncharacteristically serious eye. "Are you sure you're ready for this party? I got caught up in the fun of it, but if you have any reservations, or change your mind, you know it'll be okay."

Elizabeth was thoughtful before speaking. "I'll explain it later, but things feel different. It's part of my moving forward. Peter says I'm making progress and this feels right. It's about learning to do the things that scare me." Elizabeth smiled. "I owe you everything—you are an earth angel, Marni." She contemplated the word, "angel," and marveled at how many meanings that word held for her.

Marni smiled and gave her friend a hug. "You're coming right along. Must be all that good therapy and meds." She looked up when two steaming mugs were placed on the counter in front of them. "I love the job of getting you into the social world again. Who knows. Maybe we won't lose you after all to the beautiful people in California." Marni's conversational patter was usually glib and Elizabeth was used to it so she did not react other than a slightly perceptible eye roll.

The two women popped off the stools and took their coffees to the condiment area. "You can always give us a sign or an elbow, or whatever, if it gets too weird. Josh and I get it."

૪ ૪ ૪

Elizabeth considered taking an anxiety pill while she was waiting for Marni and Josh to pick her up, but she resisted the urge. Doug and Jenna and the kids had gone Christmas shopping leaving her alone to get ready for her first social outing since Thanksgiving. Listening to and trusting that now familiar inner voice, she looked at herself in the decorative mirror inside the entry and put her hand to her cheek. Her color was good and she had gained a few pounds that filled her out. It was all due to Doug, Marni, her faithful support teams, and The Watchers whose presence was merely a breath away. The Bauer project had gone well, and she was given the option of working on a larger one in progress after the first of the year. But, Elizabeth leaned toward being with her new-found family as the better choice to move her into the future.

The sparkle of red shoes drew her attention and she wiggled her toes enjoying how good they felt. The shoes were symbolic of a new beginning, and she fully realized that "now" was all there is or could ever be. She pulled her white merino coat out of the closet and slid it over the white dress and assessed her whole image with a smile of approval. The phone in her purse buzzed. She lifted it out of her bag and retrieved a text from Marni. She and Josh were running late. Elizabeth went to the couch and turned on the TV. She did not want to over-think about what might unfold in the hours to come. Her nerves might win.

It was an upscale holiday party in a restaurant reserved exclusively for their group. Marni's cousin, Mark, was hosting it at one of the city's high-rise fine dining establishments. Many of the same folks Elizabeth met at Thanksgiving would be there and she knew Marni's extended family threw a great party. The seventeenth floor offered glittery views of a sprawling city. Boston's nighttime skyline was usually ablaze, but this was the season of light, and it pulled out all the stops.

Chapter Twenty-Three

Winter Blossoms

Aleksander Ryen worked with Marni's cousin, Mark, in a software think tank. He developed innovative systems for the automotive industry. He was introduced to Elizabeth as part of a group at the Petrakis' Thanksgiving event, and inquired about her, but Mark supplied sketchy information about Elizabeth's circumstances regarding the sudden loss of her husband earlier in the year and her attempted suicide. Aleksander surmised the timing wasn't right and backed off the notion of approaching her. He didn't want to jeopardize a potential relationship and he was in the midst of resolving complicated romance issues of his own. But kismet persisted. When he left the Petrakis' after the holiday dinner, he nearly ran into a Mercedes in the driveway and saw Elizabeth again. She glanced his way from the backseat, and when their eyes connected, he knew he had to meet this woman. He accepted that everyone had baggage, and that Elizabeth was not in the dating game yet, so this party would be a perfect venue for a casual way to get acquainted.

❧ ❧ ❧

The swift upshot of the elevator to the seventeenth floor was not the only reason Elizabeth's stomach was queasy. Her considerations about readiness to do social things battled with her nerves. "Mind if I stick close for a while?" she asked Marni.

"It'll all come back to you." Marni checked her hair in the reflection of the window glass that surrounded the entry of the high-rise restaurant then turned to her friend. "You look amazing, Liz. Everything's cool."

"They're a great crowd," Josh said, and winked at Marni before they made their entrance.

"Hey, guys! Welcome! Merry Christmas! How's it goin', cuz?" Mark hugged Marni then turned to Elizabeth and gave her a quick hug, too. "We met at Thanksgiving, right?" His smile was charming to the nth. "Glad you could make it." Mark ushered them inside to the gathering area. A sheet of floor-to-ceiling windows filled with sparkling lights from the city below served as a backdrop and appeared to stretch for miles into the night. Cool jazz played seasonal songs that spilled out from speakers, as Mark pointed to a pony wall where a linen-draped table was set up with an open bar. Wine glasses piled into a pyramid served both functional and aesthetic purposes. Bartenders and servers were at hand. "The bar's over there and a buffet's in the corner. You can hang your wraps in the coat room off the entrance." He gestured to his right.

Elizabeth couldn't believe she did not remember meeting Mark at Thanksgiving. He was a hybrid of Greek god and geek god, and she saw instantly the family charisma and physical resemblance to Marni. The two women wandered into an open area with indirect lighting and placed their coats on hangers and filed them next to others on a long garment rod.

"Let's find the champagne—I'm ready to eat anything that doesn't move," Marni said, after she shed her wrap. She exited the room and linked arms with Josh who waited for her outside the door.

"Do the things that scare me the most." Elizabeth said to herself, as she followed behind Marni and Josh. The trio meshed into a sea of people who were eating, drinking and embroiled in conversations.

Trays of champagne flutes were placed around on glass tables with uplights and Marni scooped up two glasses and handed one to Elizabeth. "To new beginnings," Marni clinked Elizabeth's glass and turned to find Josh who had wandered over to the bar and was ordering a margarita.

Elizabeth made her way to the buffet. The tummy butterflies had disappeared and growls of hunger took their place after a few sips of champagne and inhaling the delicious aromas that wafted up from the steam tables. She looked over the array of food items and picked up a plate and tableware. After taking a modest sampling from each pan, she juggled her glass and plate and looked around for a place to sit. She spotted a gray suede-covered ottoman near the windows with the stunning views and made her way to claim it. She set her flute on a side table and eased onto the edge of the tufted cushion, eager to get something into her stomach. It was not as bad as she had anticipated and she savored the first few bites of a crab cake. Eat first, mix later. She had never been good at cocktail conversation, introverts struggle with it, but hoped the champagne would help, as she took a healthy swallow of the bubbly to wash down a bite of salad. There was something comforting about the social ritual. And for some reason, she had a good feeling deep under the layers of fear, but was afraid to admit it. This glittery night view made her feel close to Metatron and Sandalphon and believed they would approve of her stepping out of her grief and into a new experience. Through her encounters with them, she emerged as a renewed human being after nearly leaving this world.

Mesmerized by the jaw-dropping view and holiday atmosphere, Elizabeth did not hear Aleksander approach. He extended a flute of champagne to her. "I noticed your glass was empty and this is, after all, a party." Elizabeth found herself transfixed by the transparent blue of his eyes, as she accepted the glass.

"Aleksander Ryen. I work with Mark. And you must be Elizabeth," he added confidently with a boyish smile.

"I am." Elizabeth was jarred into the here and now and scooted over to make a place for him to sit. "This view is amazing. What a great spot for a restaurant. Food's really good, too." She sipped her drink and picked at a ravioli on her plate, but managed to return his genuine smile. The silence was awkward until she found her voice. She kept reminding herself to stretch and do the fearful thing. Risk and see what happens. After all, Peter said the flip side to fear was excitement and she was about to find out if that was true.

"I remember you from Thanksgiving, but I don't think we met officially. That was quite an event—Marni's lucky to have such a large caring family." A silence seemed to stretch forever and Elizabeth wished he would say something.

"I asked Mark about meeting you then, but the timing wasn't right. I can tell you are in a better place—and for that matter, so am I. Timing, as they say, is everything. Let's toast to that." Aleksander nudged his glass toward hers and they clinked. His aqua-blue eyes were luminous, as he assessed every square inch of her face. "And, please, call me Alek."

Elizabeth was warm and alive with the effects of the champagne and a connection to another human being that had been dormant too long. Time split in two and she was transported to another place that kindled a spark of passion that Metatron had spoken of after the meeting with Stephen. The white light had cleansed and prepared her for another path, another dimension to her life. The door was open and she had but to walk through it.

Marni and Josh finished filling their plates and looked around for a table. Marni caught sight of Alek and Elizabeth perched comfortably on the ottoman, and squeezed Josh's arm. "Oh my God, Josh. Look at that. I thought she was hiding in the bathroom or something. They don't see anything else but each other." Tears filled Marni's eyes while she steered her companion to a pair of empty chairs at a round table within view of her friend. "There really may be a God."

≫ ≫ ≫

Elizabeth and Aleksander continued to talk without interruption. The ease of their exchange was the first blush of a relationship taking root.

"I was the one who nearly hit your car in the driveway after Thanksgiving. Didn't think before pulling out which is not a great way to make an impression, but there you were in the backseat and I knew I had to meet you." Alek revealed. "Mark talked to Marni and she thought this party might make a good litmus test," he looked down then up at her.

"I'm not sure whether to be mad or flattered. Marni's heart is in the right place and I owe her everything. Including my life." The heaviness of her statement penetrated the mood for an instant. "That's a story for another time." Elizabeth searched the room to find her friend and saw Marni and Josh kibitzing with a small group of people near the bar. "Speaking of Marni, mind if we join them?"

Alek took her hand and pulled her to her feet and she stood beside him for the first time. They were the perfect height for each other. Alek was taller than Stephen, but somehow it was right.

"Hey, Liz." Marni scooped her friend into a sideway hug. "I see you and Alek are acquainted," her smile devilish.

Elizabeth tried to appear casual, but the blotches on her neck and cheeks matched her shoes. "Yes, we are," subtly elbowing Marni's arm.

Alek stood behind Elizabeth and put his hands on her shoulders. He whispered in her ear, "What can I get you? Another drink, coffee or should I surprise you?"

"Surprise me," she said, looking straight at Marni with a look of an infatuated woman.

Chapter Twenty-Four

Crossroads

The rustic decor of the Ale House Restaurant, a converted salt cellar-style historic house in downtown New Bristol, was authentic and oozed an otherworldly charm. Elizabeth and Alek sat across from her brother and Jenna and studied the Bill of Fare menus based on typical 1756 cuisine, but adapted to modern tastes. Blood pudding did not sound appetizing, but the mutton stew or shepherd's pie was doable. It was difficult to read the menu under the flame of one beeswax taper and the minuscule light from the narrow windows at that time of day and year, but eventually the foursome made their culinary decisions.

Meeting Elizabeth's family was a big step and Alek had been warned Doug was overly protective and an astute attorney. "Does a bottle of Malbec sound good?" Alek graciously offered hoping to impress Doug.

"Let's get a bottle of white and red. Pinot Gris?" Doug asked with a tinge of one-upmanship to his tone of voice.

Alek called for the waitperson, a buxom wench in full tavern costume of the period. She approached Alek and bent over with her abundant breasts at his eye level.

Doug watched to see if Alek would get lost in the woman's cleavage spilling out of her laced corset, but he was not distracted. Alek only had eyes for Elizabeth.

The day before Doug and Jenna were to leave for California, Elizabeth and her brother took a walk in a neighborhood park and stopped near a statue of a Revolutionary War hero. They were virtually alone due to a surge of bitter chill that had dropped down from the North across the Great Lakes. Not having gloves, Doug kept his hands in the pockets of a parka that belonged to Stephen, while Elizabeth floated easily in a full length down coat with heavy knit cap and scarf, her boots crunching the frozen remnants of dead leaves.

"I'm only postponing it, Doug." She walked backwards staring at her sibling straight on.

"I get it, but you don't know much about this guy, Alek. He seemed ok, but I'm skeptical. Don't you think it's too soon? Give yourself some time and space not to mention some warmth! California is the best this time of year."

Elizabeth could not go into the reasons why, but she knew she had Stephen's permission to cherish their memories, and go forward and make new ones; to move on with her life, no matter how it looked to anyone else.

"I'll come out this summer when the kids are out of school. It'll give me time to get the house in shape, because I intend to sell it when the market perks up in spring. There's a long list of things to upgrade and repairs that need attention between now and then. I wasn't thinking clearly when I said I would visit now."

Doug glanced up to see a few errant flakes drift to the ground and he picked up his pace. "Looks like we're about to get that snow."

"Please don't worry. If anything goes sideways, I promise to call and not have a repeat meltdown performance. I'm feeling like a new woman, thanks to you and Jenna and the kids. I know I have a real family now." She put her arm through Doug's and snuggled close. "I promise."

They resumed their walk and turned a corner and disappeared down a path as the snow began to stick.

🕊 🕊 🕊

The Mercedes was packed and Jenna checked the kids to make sure they were strapped into their seats and had their last-minute belongings secured.

The snow left slush on the driveway, yard and roads and it glistened blinding white in the brilliant sun. Elizabeth brought out luggage and Christmas gift bags and helped stow them in the car. When Jenna's final check yielded an okay sign, Doug slammed the trunk lid and the trio stood together by the side of the car.

"I'll miss you and cannot imagine how I'll repay you for everything you've done. I know the sacrifices you've made, and . . ." Hot tears spilled down Elizabeth's cheeks. She blotted her face and nose with a tissue and squinted in the sun, as she peered into the backseat and waved good-bye and blew kisses to her niece and nephew.

Doug gathered Jenna and his sister into a giant bear hug. "Love you, Liz. We're holding you to a summer visit." Doug and Jenna both wiped their eyes. "Hope you're doing the right thing. Take it slow." Doug opened the car door and Jenna waved as she went to the passenger side and slid into her seat.

Doug gave his sister one final squeeze and quickly got into the driver's seat and started the engine. Sun flashed off chrome, as he pulled out of the driveway. Elizabeth stood by the front door wiping her eyes with the cuff of her sweater until they were out of sight then disappeared inside.

Chapter Twenty-Five

New Brooms

Elizabeth swiped the screen on her cell checking the calendar pages then conducted several Google searches. She made notes on the tradespeople she would need to hire for the renovations and repairs on her house and compiled a list of solid candidates and times she could meet with them before she called. The house felt empty and the quiet was a stark reminder of her situation. A familiar sinking feeling re-surfaced and she decided to fire up her playlist to shift her mood when the doorbell rang. She got up from her desk chair and hobbled toward the door, attempting to pump blood into the leg she was sitting on.

Looking through the peephole, she observed Mrs. Goldstein bundled up in a bulky jacket on the porch with a package in her arms.

"Mrs. Goldstein! Welcome home. I thought you weren't coming back til spring. Is everything okay? Come in!"

Inside the foyer, she handed Elizabeth a large crumpled brown sack printed with a logo that read, "Sabra's Bazaar—Istanbul, Turkey."

"For you, my dear," she said, peeling off her wool jacket and hand-knitted scarf hanging them on one of the coat hooks lining the wall. "Oh, Mr. Goldstein and I are fine. He was eager to get home, worried about the pipes freezing and his garden plants. Oy, the man does not know how to relax!"

Elizabeth smiled, graciously accepted the gift and ushered Mrs. Goldstein into the living room. Both sat down and Elizabeth immediately unwrapped the package.

"It's Christmas all over again. You didn't need to do this, but oh, my what have we here?" She examined the individually wrapped cups and samovar. "A Turkish coffee set! You knew I wouldn't have anything like this! How did you manage to get this home?"

"It was something I thought you might like . . . have you ever had Turkish coffee?"

"Not in a while, but looks like I'll learn how to make it now. Thank you," she was genuinely touched by her neighbor's generosity and got up and gave her a mooshy hug.

Admiring the set, as she unwrapped each piece and placed it on the coffee table, she quizzed Mrs. Goldstein about her trip. Her neighbor inquired about Elizabeth's holidays and the two got caught up on the more mundane aspects of life.

"There's something else," Elizabeth started. "I've met someone."

Mrs. Goldstein lit up. "You have the look. I thought to myself she's different, healthier and has the glow. Tell me, what's he like?" she sat back into her chair and pushed up the sleeves of the cardigan covering her fleshy arms.

"I thought in case you see someone here, or something, you should know. His name is Alek and works with Marni's cousin. Computer software. We actually met briefly last Thanksgiving, but I obviously wasn't ready, but think I am now."

"From the look of you, you are. Tell me, would Stephen approve? I believe we can ask and the departed will speak to us." Mrs. Goldstein cast a probing eye, as she tested Elizabeth's receptivity.

Elizabeth debated whether to reveal her experience with Stephen and in fact the whole incident of her near-death ordeal. It appeared as if Mrs. Goldstein opened the door for a discussion. "I'm certain he would." Elizabeth stood up and offered to help her neighbor out of the chair. "Do you have time for tea? Maybe save Turkish coffee for after I learn how to make it?"

Without a word, Mrs. Goldstein bustled toward the kitchen.

Elizabeth piled the cups, spoons and plates into the sink after laying out the saga of her near-death experience, the angelic Watchers and being with Stephen. "There you have it. I'm not sure what it means except I know there is something more—spiritual to life. I feel as if I have been transformed, changed in a way I can't explain. I believe I have a second chance to make something of my life. I didn't tell my brother about the experience or Stephen's blessing and that it postponed going to California until summer. I told him I wanted to fix up the house, get repairs and maintenance done first."

"My dear Elizabeth, we should all be so blessed to have a second chance at anything in life. I believe you believe your experience."

Elizabeth appreciated her warm maternal gaze.

"I look forward to meeting your young man. I'm nearly family now that you've shared these details of your near passing and the journey you went on."

Elizabeth's phone buzzed in her pocket and she answered.

"Hey, Liz. Fred here."

"I need to take this. It's my boss."

Mrs. Goldstein finished tidying up and whispered she would let herself out and they waved each other good-bye and Elizabeth continued her conversation.

"I've got good news," Fred said, "how does taking on the Bauer account full-time sound?"

Elizabeth paused. "Let me get back to you, Fred. Thanks, but I'll have to let you know tomorrow." She ended the call as anxiety and anticipation tangled in knots in her gut.

Looking around for something red to incubate her entrance into The Watcher's realm, she knew this called for Sandalphon and Metatron to help and maybe Stephen who had appeared as a vague specter in her dreams lately, alerting her that change was in the wind and would affect not only her career, but the whole direction of her life.

Chapter Twenty-Six

Full Circles

Closing the door to Peter Candless' office for the last time felt like a metaphor for Elizabeth closing that chapter in her life. She exited through the hallway and out into the open air feeling confident and reassured by her therapist that she was healthy enough to function well on her own. He was pleased with her judgement and ability to make decisions during the last few months, and left the therapy door open on an "as needed" basis for when life presented its inevitable stressors.

The sun and mild temperatures were a surprise the first week in February and the harbingers of an early spring. As Elizabeth traversed the hospital campus working her way toward Sister Antoinette's a few blocks away, she took in the air tinged with that indescribable something that heralded the transition from one season to the next. Her instincts energized her, as she gingerly approached the Sister's living quarters. The porch was swept and all dead leaves and debris of the past winter were gone awaiting the new foliage and flowers that would soon flourish in the lovely cement urns on each side of the pillars.

Elizabeth remembered her trepidation and, yes, fear, when she was there last fall. The charge of that event had dissipated and was replaced with the hope of new beginnings, something she could never have imagined then. She waited for the nun in the reception area, barely seated before Sister Antoinette greeted her.

"My dear Elizabeth. How well you look!" The Sister's words were genuine.

"And you, as well, Sister. Thank you for taking time to see me."

"It's so lovely out, would you like to walk and visit outdoors? We have a charming courtyard with benches in the back which is private or we can just stroll the grounds."

The two ventured out into the late winter sun.

※ ※ ※

So much has happened since we last talked, Sister. I really don't know where to start—I can give you the highlights, and I promised to tell you about the rest of my vision." Elizabeth let the statement hang in the glorious air.

"Highlights first." Despite her hefty size, Sister Antoinette kept up a steady pace and her demeanor was more casual. Elizabeth was thankful for both.

"Today was my last session with Peter. He's been an amazing guide to insights I would never have discovered on my own. He left the option of seeing him again open so that I won't get to the low point I did last year when Stephen . . ." Elizabeth was surprised how his name sounded when she said it out loud. Last year it would have evoked a piercing sadness, but now it was like talking about an old friend she had just recently spent time with.

"You have come a long way. I couldn't be more pleased. It validates that God hears our prayers," Antoinette said, with a sidelong glance at her friend.

"Through this tragedy, my spiritual side has definitely been awakened." Elizabeth's bright smile reassured the nun of its veracity. The two meandered toward the side gate to the convent, and just like The Secret Garden, a cherished book from Elizabeth's youth, they entered a storybook setting surrounded by original walls. Ivy and moss covered the bricks and Elizabeth wondered how long this quaint part of Americana would be allowed to stand without tearing it down and blending it with the sleek concrete structures erected around it on the medical campus. Perhaps the influence of the Church was strong enough to curtail it.

"This is my favorite bench where I often pray." Antoinette rustled to an ornately carved wooden bench underneath a barren elm. "It's delightful in the summer when it's hot and the tree is a leafy umbrella of shade, but today the sunlight is welcome."

Sitting side by side, Antoinette smoothed her skirts and turned directly to Elizabeth. "I'm anxious to hear how your experience has, uhm, affected your life. Are you aware the beings who greeted you when you were unconscious and near death were only whispered about in the ancient scrolls and were kept from our version of the Bible?" Antoinette leaned closer to Elizabeth and lowered her voice. "It's blasphemous for me to entertain any of this, but I believe you believe your experience was real. Over the years in my counseling capacity I've been privy to similar accounts, but yours is elaborate and . . . hauntingly authentic to the ancient texts."

Elizabeth registered surprise at the nun's candor and knowledge, and was emboldened by it. "As I've explained, the color red triggers an altered state where I'm drawn in to the realm of The Watchers. I recently revisited the indigo field which was preparation for walking into the white light that was indescribable." Elizabeth, eyes shut, reflected on the image of traveling through the inky realm and into the burst of white vibrating light out of which emerged her beloved Stephen.

Antoinette, rapt, barely breathing, hung her attention on every word uttered from the young woman next to her.

Elizabeth relayed the warmth of her husband's embrace and her desire to be with him forever, rejecting his insistence that her life was just beginning without him. Stephen convinced her that she had a destiny to fulfill—one that was not clear now, but one that would be revealed. She would have to trust.

Elizabeth's throat tightened, suppressing a lump of emotion. After a pause, as if watching a movie in her mind, her voice softened when she added, "He assured me I would inherit a "knowing" that would help me find the right path."

"And you made the choice to return to your life here."

Antoinette's empathy surprised Elizabeth.

"Has the 'knowing' happened? Those who have similar testimonies have gone on to live out their destinies with surprising results. The twists and plots of God's plan for us is a mystery revealed in plain sight, if we would pay attention." Antoinette fingered the crucifix resting on her chest.

Elizabeth noticed the nun appeared less tense now that she was assured her journey was on the side of the good versus evil. The profundity of Antoinette's words sunk in. "I'm grateful my experience confirmed your suspicions about The Watchers."

Antoinette nodded and Elizabeth was validated.

"I believe they're my guides, and I couldn't separate myself from them even if I wanted to. They showed me an ancient book where my life path was written. It tracks every soul who has ever lived, and if it is written, it is cast. This has been hard to take in, but it helps me understand everything that's happened. It's like finding the missing pieces to a giant cosmic jigsaw puzzle."

"And did they tell you anything specific about your future?" Her question indicated she knew what was on Elizabeth's heart.

"Doug wanted me to go to California after the holidays, but I thought summer would be better because I've decided to sell my house and by delaying the trip, it will give me time to fix it up and market it," Elizabeth avoided eye contact by looking anywhere but at Antoinette's piercing gaze, "and I've met someone special. I want to see where this relationship goes." Elizabeth shifted around and took in a deep breath. "And, I've signed another design contract that was too good to pass up." Elizabeth looked into the nun's face and observed it had softened considerably since their first meeting. "Stephen and the twin Watchers have come to me in my dreams after making these decisions and they affirmed that I have chosen well. Metatron says in the end we all have free will."

"And such a gift we were given." Antoinette sighed with relief and looked pleased. "With that, I think we should have tea." She rose without waiting for Elizabeth's reply.

Chapter Twenty-Seven

Paths and Purposes

The carpenters were late again and Elizabeth was irritated. She had lunch planned with Marni who she had not seen in weeks due to the renovations on her home and the overtime she was accruing on the Bauer project. Housebound with her job and now with the tradespeople who had a different drumbeat than hers, she patched through a call and before it could connect, she saw the white pickup with "Clover Construction" in kelly-green lettering pull in her driveway. She opened the front door and without smiling motioned to Sean. He approached the porch.

"I thought you were supposed to be here at nine? I have an appointment and need to leave. Those window sills have to be finished today because the painters are scheduled . . ."

Sean, an Irishman in his mid-forties with hands that looked like he worked in the trades, held one up stopping her affront and grinned an Irish smile that oozed with Celtic charm. His partner set up the ladders and pulled toolboxes from the truck bed and opened them and started up the rungs. "We'll take care of ya . . . ya just go on to yer meetin' and we'll call ya if we run into any problems."

With her anger diffused, Elizabeth donned her jacket and locked up the house, grateful that the predictions for an early spring were proving to be true by the feel of the mild air.

Marni took the day off work and invited Elizabeth to her place. A clear glass vase with a spray of daffodils punctuated the center of the dining room table and visually complemented the wooden bowl of tossed spring greens with slices of grilled chicken on top. The aroma of fresh bread welcomed Elizabeth when Marni opened her apartment door.

"It's about time you came out of your lair! Too early for chardonnay?" Marni grabbed her friend's arm and ushered her to the kitchen.

After lunch, Marni nestled into a pillowed niche on her couch and Elizabeth carried her wine glass to the brown faux suede side chair, sat down and propped her feet up on the matching ottoman. "I feel like I'm ditching school, not that I ever did . . ." Elizabeth smiled a little wickedly. "Lunch was great. I didn't realize how much I needed a pleasure pause."

"I thought Alek was keeping you busy?" Marni asked.

"We're both on a fast track these days, but things should lighten up with the house projects almost done." Elizabeth's color rose. "Things are good with us—I just want to take it slow."

"Because?" Marni asked.

"I made a promise to Doug. It may take a while, but we'll get there," Elizabeth said.

"You've come a long way, Liz." Marni smiled, adjusted the pillows behind her back and curled one of her springy ringlets around her finger. "Believe it or not, things are getting serious with Josh. For real. I never thought I'd say this, but I can't imagine life without him."

"If it can happen for you, there's hope." Elizabeth lifted her glass in the air toward her friend and took a dainty sip of crisp white wine and paused until the silence made her uncomfortable.

"Thanks for today. I know you haven't wanted to hear about what happened when I was declared clinically dead, but it's been a year since Stephen's passing and I've so wanted to share with you how it tied in with my experience. And the dreams . . ." Elizabeth measured the response of her friend's body language. "I even told the rest of the story to Sister Antoinette and we bonded in a strange sort of way—it opened up a spiritual world I never knew existed and she shed light on the whole phenomenon. It's apparently not uncommon and she's seen it before only mine was, well, different." Elizabeth tested Marni's receptivity by observing her reaction. Whether it was the wine or the solid relationship she had with her guy, she wasn't sure, but Marni looked interested and didn't change the subject.

"Shoot. I can be open-minded. I see so much change in you that there has to be something to it."

Elizabeth described meeting Metatron and Sandalphon and the grandeur of the multi-colored realms. In re-telling the story, Elizabeth found herself transported to each place by intricately detailing the amazing beauty and mystery of the places where The Watchers dwell.

"When I was able to remember the last part, or be ready for it, I entered a place of white light where I met Stephen. Marn, he was as vibrant and whole and fully alive as I remembered him." Elizabeth shut her eyes and mentally revisited the warmth of his embrace and communion with his essence.

"I absolutely knew I had a choice." Elizabeth leaned forward in her chair for emphasis. "Marni, I chose to come back, to return to this life. I have been told by the twin angels that there is a purpose for every soul and that . . ."

Marni shifted and stretched her legs, as if she was about to stand. "I don't know what to say, Liz. My God, I could never imagine going through what you did. I'm sorry I wasn't receptive. I just, well, am not too much into this religious thing."

I wouldn't have believed it either, but the more I share and read about it, I'm finding out what an incredible gift I've been given."

"So, tell me about your dreams. Do you go back there?" Marni swirled her wine in the glass and looked at her friend through the crystal.

"Metatron told me to concentrate on the color red to re-enter the first realm, but now I find I can slip into the white light through my dreams where the angels and Stephen are. They've been telling me I'm moving in the right direction. I don't know how it works, but I'm able to "know" things without understanding how I know them." Elizabeth raised both hands palms up and shrugged. "It's hard to explain."

"What does moving in the right direction look like?" Marni planted her elbows on her knees, genuinely interested.

"As much as I want to be with Doug and Jenna and am grateful for their support, California doesn't feel like where I'm supposed to be. Maybe for a visit, but not a permanent move." Elizabeth leaned toward friend. "Marni, I know I need to sell my house and there will be a new chapter if I do. Like, I know Alek and I were meant to meet, but I have kept him at a distance because I wasn't clear about a relationship. Stephen came to me in a dream and told me to let go of the past and appreciate our miraculous years together, because it was a preparation for a different relationship that awaits. One that will take me in directions I've yet to imagine. I don't know if it's Alek—he may be foreshadowing something else. Heady stuff." Elizabeth delivered a long sigh before she stood and stretched her lithe limbs.

"Amen, sister, on that!" Marni replied.

Both women were quiet for several minutes reflecting on the conversation.

"Let's change it up. Go play. This is pretty intense for me." Marni uncurled her legs.

"Anything in mind? Liz asked.

"Since we're both delinquents today, how about whipping out your credit card at the mall, then going to a club or a movie or?"

"You always were a bad influence." Liz grinned good-naturedly and popped out of the chair. "I'll feel too guilty of we don't clean up the lunch stuff first." She scooped up her glass and dishes on the table and put them into the kitchen sink and ran water over them.

"Do you ever just let go and get crazy?" Marni chided her.

"I have faith you'll make sure I do." Elizabeth said to her friend, as she wiped down the countertops.

Chapter Twenty-Eight

Twilight Time

A Mapletown Realty sign swayed in its bracket on Elizabeth's lawn. The shutters and sills were freshly painted a majestic plum color that complemented the soft dove gray of the body of the house. Elizabeth's artistic eye was at work with every detail of the renovation and upgrades.

Elizabeth was at the curb retrieving mail from her mailbox when she heard Mrs. Goldstein open her door.

"Yoo-hoo!" Mrs. Goldstein came out on her porch and waved.

"Hi, Mrs. Goldstein," Elizabeth said, as she approached the porch holding a wad of envelopes and junk mail in her hand. "Such a waste of paper. I wish I could get off these lists, but guess if you have an address that's impossible."

"Can you come in for a minute?" Mrs. Goldstein's apron had flour on it and tantalizing aromas drifted through the open door. "I just made matzah ball soup and have plenty. Would you like some?"

"What will I do without you for a neighbor?" Elizabeth asked.

"Come in and I'll get you a container for your supper." Mrs. Goldstein and Elizabeth trundled inside.

The Goldstein's home exuded a kitschy-ness from a past era. At Mrs. Goldstein's insistence, Elizabeth sat down on an overstuffed floral settee. The whole room was rendered in shades of pink which created an oddly comforting glow. Elizabeth was a captive bird in Mrs. Goldstein's cage.

"Have you had any nibbles on your house?" The woman stood in the doorway and wiped the bottom of a Tupperware container with her apron. Crossing the room, she sat the soup on a doily coaster already on the maple coffee table in front of the settee.

"It's been shown a couple of times, but no offers. I'm hoping there'll be more activity once spring is officially underway."

"Mr. Goldstein and I wish you'd reconsider. What about that nice boy you've been seeing? You could maybe start a family. Such a lovely little house would be perfect for that."

Elizabeth was being led into waters where she did not want to go. Mrs. Goldstein was a caring neighbor, but had a tendency to get a little close to the bone and Elizabeth's boundaries were always in jeopardy where Mrs. Goldstein was concerned.

"I need to start fresh. I couldn't possibly think about Alek or anyone else for that matter living in that house." Elizabeth bit her lip fearing she had said too much.

"Of course, I was just thinking of what a hassle it will be and—do you know where you are going to move? California?"

Elizabeth realized the woman was an expert wheedler. Time to refocus. "I'm planning on a trip to see Doug and Jenna once the house sells. That's about as far as I've gotten."

"We were thinking of remodeling our daughter's room. I may take up a hobby in my retirement and use that room. Maybe quilting, or I could start a blog or who knows? Did you like the work you had done with the folks you hired?"

Elizabeth reached for her soup and stood. "There were times when they could've been a little more efficient and punctual, but overall, the work was done right." She edged toward the front door. "I really do need to go, Mrs. Goldstein. I'll return your container tomorrow."

"Enjoy! Come over when we can talk." Mrs. Goldstein's plump rosy face was always pleasant.

Elizabeth slipped out the craftsman-style front door and waved over her shoulder fearing she would get hooked back in, if she looked back and made eye contact.

꽃 꽃 꽃

After too many hours immersed in computer work, Elizabeth got a notion to drive to New Bristol's central shopping area where quaint novelty and housewares shops that used to be called boutiques lined a treed downtown. She felt restless and followed an atypical urge to be out among people and do something she had never done—go to a psychic. She could not pinpoint the genesis of her inspiration, but knew to obey that inner prompt which surfaced more frequently these days. There was wisdom in paying attention to those inner nudges, because serendipitous events usually followed.

Despite venturing out on the edge of rush hour, she easily secured a parking spot near the Psychic Readings storefront. Robotically, she exited her vehicle, fed the meter and approached the psychic's door lined with a lacy curtain behind a pane of glass. Tibetan bells tinkled, as she turned the worn oval brass doorknob and ducked inside. A year ago she would have considered this a crazy person's lair, but not today.

Elizabeth inhaled the exotic incense that hung in the air, as she pivoted to shut the door and glanced around her. The decor was not disappointing; it was exactly as she imagined it would be. Subdued lighting and strands of blue crystal beads hung in a doorway and she thought she detected movement behind them. There were floor cushions and Persian rugs overlapping each other and a table in the center of the room with a candle glowing in the lotus-shaped holder and a deck of cards on the fringed shimmery purple silk cloth that covered the round table. Two oak chairs with deep satin cushions were positioned across from each other. Soft, almost imperceptible music glued the atmosphere together. Water cascaded down the sides of an indoor fountain and Elizabeth felt transported to another time.

A slim woman dressed in flowing garments emerged with quiet elegance through the beads and her velvety voice welcomed Elizabeth. She narrowly assessed her client with a sweep of her dark eyes under lashes too thick to be real, then smiled. "I am Charmaine. You wish a reading?" A petite hand emerged from a voluminous sleeve and she offered it to Elizabeth who registered surprise at the strength of her grip and that her skin felt hot and dry and chapped.

"Yes, I think so. I've never done this before, but I've seen your shop . . . oh, I'm Elizabeth."

Charmaine studied Elizabeth's face and gestured toward the table. The women sat down in unison, Charmaine next to the deck of cards. Elizabeth could not take her eyes off the magnetic woman across from her. She watched Charmaine shuffle the cards without a word, and with lids half-closed, she placed the cards in front of her and slipped into a trance. A considerable silence ensued where Elizabeth's heart was pounding loud enough to wake the dead. When Charmaine's lids lifted, the candle flame reflected its image in her pupils.

"You have a cloud around your heart. You have endured a great loss, but something new is stirring, a seed waiting to be germinated. I see indecision and doubt in a relationship." She picked up the deck of cards. "Let's see what the cards have to say." She placed the shuffled deck in front of Elizabeth. "Cut the cards into three stacks expressing your question or heart's desire each time."

Elizabeth contemplated what her inner desires were telling her, closed her eyes and separated the cards into piles.

The reader turned over the first stack. "This is your past." She paused and turned over the middle stack, "This is your present." She studied the cards facing up then, as she turned over the third stack to her right, she leveled a piercing look at Elizabeth, "This is your future."

Elizabeth felt suddenly cold when she uttered the words.

Charmaine absent-mindedly clasped the crystal sphere pendant that hung on a fine silver chain between her breasts and pointed to the pile of cards on her left. "You have been through great trials, here, in your past, there is The Tower. It is a Major Arcana card meaning it was written in your destiny. Something you must experience in this lifetime. You have recently been through upside down change, conflict, but the disruption will bring enlightenment. Do you understand what this means?"

Elizabeth's eyes were wide and fixed on Charmaine, as she shook her head yes. "Yes, my husband died suddenly and I, uh, did not want to go on."

Charmaine smiled and swept a strand of hair away from her face. "And you came through stronger and had amazing experiences on the journey. Tell me, are you strengthened, is your soul restored?"

"Yes, but I'm conflicted. I'm afraid to trust between what I feel and what I know. I have family who wants me with them, but this is my home and I have met someone. That's why I'm here. I thought you could see something I can't. What'll be the right choice." Elizabeth leaned forward preparing to hang on every word from the reader.

"You want clarity. You asked for clarity. Any path you choose now will bring its own rewards. There is no wrong answer." Charmaine tapped the center card. "The Knight of Wands here is an energetic young man who can be a friend or lover with a dark side, but can he can also represent the coming and going of a matter. I feel certain that which you have been through is over and a smorgasbord of possibilities await you."

Elizabeth adjusted her cushion and sat back relieved. "What is the future card?"

"The Ten of Cups. It portends lasting happiness. Perfection in human and Divine love." The candle flame flickered. "It is your future, Elizabeth."

Elizabeth imagined the incense amplified and the twang of the sitar grew bolder. In fact, the atmosphere was close and cloying and she craved fresh air. She gazed at the woman across the table whose red velvet headband looked psychedelic, vibrating in the semi-darkness. She could not take her eyes off it and felt a presence, being drawn through the familiar portal where Metatron waited in his bright crimson robe.

Chapter Twenty-Nine

Finding Home

Flight 627 to Los Angeles was fully booked. Elizabeth inched her way down the aisle, bodies pressing her from behind, as she searched for her seat number and an empty space in an overhead compartment. She lifted her bag into an available space and found her seat a few rows forward, eased into it, grateful that it was on the inside aisle.

She stood to let a lean nerdy young man in his twenties maneuver across to his seat by the window and stood again for the matronly woman who would occupy the center seat to her left. Flushed and nervous, eyes darting and fussing with her handhelds, she attempted to cram her purse and carry-on under the seat in front of her, but Elizabeth could clearly see one of them would have to be stowed overhead.

"Excuse me, would you like me to find a place for your tote? I don't think it will fit there." The woman looked relieved, the tension released on her face, and nodded. "Why, yes, thank you, dear." She yanked one end of the bulky bag and extracted it, then handed it to Elizabeth who deftly rearranged pieces of luggage in the compartment a few rows up on the opposite side of the cabin and inserted the carry-on where it fit perfectly.

"Do you fly often?" the woman asked.

"Not often, but enough to be familiar with the routines," Elizabeth replied. It was hard to tell the age of her seatmate, as her skin was porcelain-like except for scrawly laugh lines around her eyes and mouth and a barely perceptible double chin. Her eyes were a dark China blue and slightly disarming.

Elizabeth thought she must have been a stunner as a younger version. "Do you live here or are you visiting?"

"I didn't introduce myself—I'm Dehlia Townsend. I live with my son near New Bristol. And you?" Her warmth invited Elizabeth to engage.

"Really? I live in New Bristol. I'm on my way to visit my brother and his family to see if the grass is greener on the West Coast, or something like that. In fact, my house just sold last month and I'm sort of in-between homes right now. I rented a condo month-to-month in New Bristol which is an adjustment after being a home owner." Elizabeth was amazed how easy, almost too easy, it was to talk with this woman, as if she was an old friend. "I'm originally from Southern California, and it's been over ten years since . . ."

The lady, mid-sixties, well-groomed, but dated in a pink ruffled blouse, brown trousers and low pumps, busied herself with snugging her seatbelt. "Well, my daughter Nicole lives in the South Bay area and it's beautiful there, but I prefer my small-town life and wouldn't leave if it weren't for her."

Elizabeth secured her belt and opened her zippered tote to find her iPod. "I'm not sure where I'll be this time a year from now. I'm sort of leaving it up to the universe."

Dehlia smiled and nodded as if she caught the drift of the inference. Elizabeth installed her earbuds ready to curb any further surface conversation. She wanted to settle in and "om" to her music. The habit, a reliable ritual to relax, started during those early times in therapy and it stuck. There would be ample time to chat later on during the long cross-country flight.

"What do you like to listen to?" Dehlia ventured, as she bent forward and opened her large MK purse under the seat in front of her, and pulled out a new Woman's Day and horned-rimmed readers and prepared to read it cover-to-cover.

"A little of everything . . . salsa to classical," Elizabeth said, as she wrapped her sweater around her shoulders and made a comfortable cocoon in the cramped seat and let her eyelids close.

※ ※ ※

Just outside LAX, the Captain announced the on-time arrival at Gate 3. The passengers stirred from their lethargy and prepared to disembark, as the attendants made a last run at collecting trash before landing.

The two women had enjoyed a cordial conversation after Elizabeth's nap. She learned that Dehlia had been born in Boston and lived in New Bristol. Later she moved to the small farming suburb of Gilbert and remained her entire life. Her daughter, Nicole, was in the film industry, produced small documentaries and was caught up in the L.A. scene; she was single and liked it that way. Her son, Colin, had yet to find the "right one" and moved in with her after she was widowed five years ago. He took over the family dairy farm after his dad died. The women had that in common although Elizabeth chose not to share many of the details of her untimely widowhood.

"If California doesn't work out, we should get together for lunch or tea sometime." Dehlia suggested just before they stood to gather their luggage from the overhead bins.

"Sure. I remember Gilbert as a quaint rural area. I think we passed through it when deciding where to live." Elizabeth replied, letting her voice drop off as a memory surfaced. She and Stephen had explored the area when they were young and free. She fished out her phone from her bag and entered Dehlia's contact number and said she would stay in touch.

"I hope you find your home, Elizabeth. It's key to everything in life."

Elizabeth nodded agreement and the comment sat with her until she got to the baggage carousels and spied Doug waving at her. She felt her heart beat faster and realized she'd missed him and that familiar refrain that family, as well as home, were keys to happiness kept buzzing in her head. Now it would be her job to get them to manifest together on one coast or the other.

"Hey, you look great! Good trip?" Doug asked, as he embraced his sister.

Elizabeth assessed her brother—he looked healthier and his energy was lighter. "I'm glad to be on terra firma. But look at you, a tan already? Have you been golfing or just a lot of pool time?" Elizabeth asked.

"A little of both, all in the name of business. What carousel is yours?"

Doug said, as he relieved Liz of her carry-on. They walked toward the unit that started to circulate its conveyor belt and displayed her flight number in the marquee. The bags tumbled out of the chute onto the turntable.

"There, that's it—the one with the red ribbon."

When the bag came around, Doug hoisted it off, pulled up the handle and rolled it toward the automatic glass doors. "Let's go. Traffic is more of a zoo today than usual and we have a way to go. Jenna's got a backyard BBQ planned and the kids are probably driving her nuts. They are so excited Aunt Liz is coming to visit."

Elizabeth trotted behind him, but not before catching Dehlia's eye and nodding as she wheeled her small carry-on past her trying to catch up with her attractive blonde daughter who scurried ahead toting a large bag out the glass exit doors.

"That lady lives outside New Bristol. She had the seat next to mine," Elizabeth said to Doug, as they split from the mother and daughter and went in different directions toward the parking garage. It was evident Los Angeleans operated on a fast track in every aspect of their lives. She wondered if she could adapt even for the few weeks she would be there.

❧ ❧ ❧

June in Southern California was as close to ideal as you could order it. The weather and lifestyle were the quintessential reasons the population burgeoned after the Second World War and brought it to its current status of eight-lane freeways and one of the world's largest and most diverse population centers. Elizabeth pondered how she could have been born into such an environment when every cell in her being screamed formality and resonated to a slower rhythm in the pulse of life.

Doug made several turns in the maze of a plush housing development and eventually stopped at an imposing hacienda-style villa that looked like it sprawled on several acres. "Home. Not bad—an hour and forty-five minutes."

"I forgot that everything's measured in time not distance here." Elizabeth got out of the car and panned a view of the house when Channing and Jackson bolted out the front door running toward her.

They chimed "Aunt Liz" together and ran to hug her.

"Look at you two! I don't see you for a few months and you've grown at least a foot!"

"Who wants to help?" Doug asked, as he lifted the trunk lid.

Jackson raced to the back of the Mercedes, pulled out the carry-on, plopped it on the ground and rolled it toward the entrance. Liz trailed behind Jackson and Jenna appeared in the arched doorway. They reached out to each other for hugs and she caught a glimmer of what it might be like if she called L.A. home.

Chapter Thirty

The Next Leg of the Journey

It remained pleasantly warm after the sun went down. The kids paddled and splashed in the turquoise backyard pool while Elizabeth, Doug and Jenna relaxed on chaises watching them.

"Do they ever run out of energy?" Liz asked?

"Rarely, but looks like they're winding down. This is usual for our summer evenings now that school's out. They'll be ready for bed soon . . . they've been super anxious for your visit so it's been a big day for them. Be prepared, they have a lot of places and treasures they want to show you. Depending on how you feel, we thought we'd go to the beach tomorrow and see how it stacks up—Pacific vs. Atlantic," Jenna said, motioning to her kids to come out of the pool.

"My memories aren't reliable—everything's changed so much," Liz said, as she sipped the last of her wine. "It's a completely different lifestyle here. I'd forgotten the perk of almost always beautiful weather."

Doug got up and grabbed the bottle of Sauvignon blanc from an ice bucket. "More wine before the water babies go to bed?"

"I'm operating on East Coast time, so think I'll join them when you put them down. It's been wonderful, but I'm drooping." Liz said, and handed her glass to Doug then slid off the lounge.

"Hey guys, time to dry off," Jenna stood and held out a colorful beach towel to each of her offspring. Jackson was cranky and pleaded just five more minutes, but after Channing toweled off and wrapped up, he took his towel and pouted while he tousled his hair dry and wiped the water off his berry-brown limbs.

"You coming, Aunt Liz?" Jackson asked, sidling up to her.

"I am! Let's go." Elizabeth cuddled the young boy, as they entered the house through the patio sliders.

❧ ❧ ❧

Earlier, she called Marni after her shower and the friends got caught up, including Marni's news about the wedding plans. Elizabeth mused about being a bridesmaid at a Greek wedding in mid-August, then her chain of thoughts turned to her modest bungalow and the people who bought it. A young couple with their first baby, a girl, fell in love with the charm of the home and neighborhood. She wondered how their lives would play out there and how the next junction in her own life would look. The Goldsteins were already smitten with the infant and babysitting, so the arrangement was ideal. When she allowed her mind to reflect on what her life was before and after losing Stephen, doubt, sadness and remorse moved through her, but falling into the rhythm of her brother's home and routines helped her ease through those feelings. She thought about Alek and her heart ached, but she knew they would be together if their relationship was real. She envisioned his face and sweet manner and longed for him, even though she had insisted for more space and he agreed to it. She thought she just needed more time.

Elizabeth was tucked into a massive mahogany sleigh bed in an opulently decorated room in burgundy and gold. She was surprised how invigorating and easy it had been in the company of her family and that the atmosphere and vibe of L.A. was not as distasteful as she remembered. She was dealing with her father's death then and had not fulfilled her New England dreams. The contrast in lifestyle was a chasm she would have to work on in order to breach.

Sleep was sudden and deep and dreams pooled into her awareness upon awakening. Strong feelings of familiarity and images of Metatron and Sandalphon hovering near the massive tomes where her name was written would linger with her throughout the day.

"Can we walk out on the pier, Mommy?" Jackson shouted from the back seat.

"We'll see. It looks crowded today now that school's out." Jenna said to her son.

"I used to coerce Doug to walk with me on the pier." Elizabeth squinted and shaded her eyes. "Hasn't changed much. I got grossed out at the bait and blood and guts and the fishy smell, but I wanted to go anyway. There was a neat concrete rotunda at the end with tourist information on the walls."

"I like to see what they're catching. One time this guy had a miniature shark in a bucket, I swear . . ." Jackson said, straining in his seatbelt to catch a glimpse of the ocean as Jenna turned a corner to find parking.

"You like gross. Gross." Channing scowled at her brother folding her arms.

"Okay guys. Let's let Aunt Liz decide. She's the one visiting and doesn't get to do this all the time." There was a minor scuffle happening between siblings, but neither Jenna nor Elizabeth looked around.

"There's a spot." Liz pointed to an empty space.

"Good eye!" Jenna said, as she bolted into the slot. "Bonus! Three-hour parking."

The foursome gathered their beach gear and trekked to an open expanse of sand about a quarter of a mile north of the pier. The Strand was heavy with foot traffic and was an inviting stretch of boulevard that paralleled the great Pacific. Jackson staked a claim near a wet patch of sand.

"We'll have to move again if we sit there . . . the tide is coming in. Find us something back there," Jenna pointed to a flat spot out of the wind, as Jackson and Channing raced in the same direction.

"Competitive, aren't they?" Liz said. "They have Doug's genes!"

"You got that right," Jenna replied with a high five to her sister-in-law.

A giant tote piled high with kids' toys weighted down a beach towel ablaze with images of tropical birds. Jackson and Channing played in the surf and

Jenna had a good view of them. She and Elizabeth chatted and absorbed the sun and fresh salt air with its unmistakable briny tang. Liz reflected on the time she went to the ocean after Stephen died and how she did not feel like the same person now. She was transformed by the near-death-experience and a tingle of excitement, hope and possibilities snaked up her spine.

"I saw a little coffee place on the other side of the Strand. Want an iced coffee or anything?" Elizabeth offered.

"Sure you don't mind? That'd be great. Make mine skinny and a double shot. That should hold me for the afternoon."

Elizabeth grabbed her wallet. "Kids want anything?" she asked and wrapped herself in a tie-dyed cover-up.

"Any fruit drink, but cola if they don't have that," Jenna suggested.

"Back in a few," she said, as she trudged up the sand embankment toward the Strand.

The pavement was hot enough underneath her flip-flops that they might melt, but they didn't. There was a line at the open-air window and she joined the queue. The back of a sleek blonde head turning away from the window caught Elizabeth's attention. She balanced a cardboard tray with two cups in it. She looked familiar and thought it was Dehlia's daughter, but then there are so many luscious blondes here, could she be sure? "Nicole?" Elizabeth ventured.

The woman spun around toward Elizabeth's direction looking puzzled, as she tried to locate the person who called her name. "I sat next to your mom on the flight out here yesterday. She said she was staying with her daughter who lived in the South Bay area. I recognized you from seeing you with her at the luggage pick-up. I'm Elizabeth Welles. What are the odds?"

"Oh, okay. I see. You have a good memory. Nicole Newcomb," she said, remaining aloof, but extended her petite well-manicured hand.

"I'm visiting my brother and his family for a few weeks. Small world that your mom lives near where I did in New Bristol." Elizabeth continued.

"Did? Are you thinking of moving here?" she asked, adjusting her sunglasses to get a better look at Elizabeth.

"I'm in transition, as they say, nothing definite." The line moved forward and Elizabeth was at the order window where the barista waited. "Say hi to your mom. Nice meeting you."

"You, as well. Enjoy your stay." Nicole waved and walked across the Strand to the corner, turned and made her way down the stairs past the lifeguard stations and disappeared.

Elizabeth carried the full tray of drinks back to the oasis of beach towels where Jenna was applying sunscreen to Channing's back and shoulders. Jackson was slathering on his own.

"That's a popular place. Had to wait in line." Elizabeth handed each of them their drinks. "You'll never believe what happened!" she said, as she maneuvered onto her towel and sat back against the sand chair, beverage in hand. "I ran into the daughter of the woman who sat next to me on the plane. Couldn't believe it. Talk about synchronicities happening in this sea of people!"

"That is weird. How'd you know it was her daughter?" Jenna asked.

"I saw her at the baggage pick-up—she's stunning, not easy to forget." Elizabeth held the cup to her cheek and let the ice cool her down before sipping from the hot-pink plastic straw. She shaded her eyes and looked out onto the horizon where there was a cloud bank forming. She could have sworn an image of Stephen's face emerged from the mist flanked by two familiar-looking angels.

Chapter Thirty-One

California Dreamin'

Elizabeth held up a filmy white dress to her chest while standing in front of a full-length mirror in her room. She had been exposed to a generous amount of sun the past few days which heightened her color and the tan looked good on her and made the white garment pop. She admired her new look that was fresh and relaxed and she had gained just enough weight to appear healthy and strong. She draped the gray-green crisscross ties across the front of the dress which gave her body definition and picked up the color of her eyes. Jenna had taken her shopping a few days ago and she was grateful, as the conservative little black dress she brought would never do in this setting.

"You ready, Liz?" Doug's voice echoed up the stairs.

"Almost. Give me a few more minutes," Elizabeth replied. She quickly pulled on the dress and adjusted its ties, then stepped into a pair of white ropey espadrilles that made her statuesque and fueled her confidence. She wiggled her toes, grateful that Jenna had talked her into painting them with a summery frosted coral polish. Quickly touching up her peachy lip gloss, she breezed out the door and caught her image in the oval mirror and noticed she was smiling.

Elizabeth observed the dynamics of her brother and Jenna from the backseat of their luxurious SUV. Her thoughts went to one of the times she and Stephen were going out to a party and how they might have looked to someone in the backseat. He or she would have seen two people joking, at ease and affectionate with each other, just like these two. Even after her angelic experiences and the emotional release after encountering Stephen in the Light, she questioned whether her path would lead her to that rare partnering again.

Doug slammed on the brakes and laid on the horn in order to avoid the car that ran the signal barreling through the intersection. Elizabeth was snapped back into reality. "Crazy S.O.B." Doug shook his fist in the direction of the errant motorist. He cautiously proceeded on the green light. "That was close. Everyone's in such a big fat hurry." Doug said, disgustingly.

"Calm down, Doug, we're ok. What a jerk." Jenna added.

"I'm not sure I could drive here. Do you ever get used to this traffic?"

"It's part of the scene—seems normal after a while. It's new to you and you're not familiar with the streets and freeway systems the way they are now. You'd get used to it," Doug said, smoothing back the side of his hair.

"If you say so." Elizabeth replied with a tentative tone in her voice. "Tell me again who will be there and what we're celebrating," Liz said.

"It's a consortium of law firms that specialize in real property issues and estate planning. Our firm founded the organization to offer a broad referral network and education resource and we just reached a goal of ten companies on board from which to draw. My partner, Jim White, suggested we host a get-together at his home to celebrate. Summer casual with principals and their families sounded better than a stuffy sit-down dinner." Doug pulled onto a side street lined with palms that reflected the stunning ambience of old Bel Air.

"A little out of my league, Doug. I'll find a quiet spot in the den or . . ." Elizabeth said, with trepidation.

"No need for that—there're a lot of folks I want to introduce you to—the more people you know, the more you'll be comfortable and think about staying. I'm not giving up on you." Jenna turned around and flashed a genuine smile.

Elizabeth gasped as the Mercedes circled the drive and stopped at the front double entry doors. The addition of valet parking was a level of sophistication that overwhelmed, never mind the imposing edifice of Italian Renaissance architecture. It was an estate.

"Doug, why didn't you give me a heads up?" Liz asked.

"All down-to-earth folks, you'll see. Besides you look great and who knows, you might make a connection, uh, for your work." Doug winked at his wife, as he handed his vehicle over to the young college-aged valet whose blonde hair was closely cropped and behavior was professional and efficient. Elizabeth wondered how guys found gigs like this.

The trio entered through the extra tall European-style mahogany front doors and gathered with other guests in the enormous black and white marble-tiled foyer. After preliminary introductions, Elizabeth shadowed Doug and Jenna, as they strolled out to the pool area where a live combo played non-descript background music and the uplighting and furnishings were exquisitely positioned for relaxed conversation. A pair of striped tents with catered food tables were set up on either side of the pool and an open bar completed the scene as Elizabeth took it all in thinking, "So this is California dreamin'?" She reflected on how different it was from the Christmas party where she met Alek.

Jenna steered her toward a group of women balancing wine glasses and plates.

"Jenna! Great outfit—how've you been?" a thirty-something woman who was lanky tall with a short-cropped designer-do said, as she gave her an air hug.

"Terrific, Deena. Hi, Crystal, Jane. You all look fabulous as usual!" Jenna said. "I'd like you to meet Doug's sister, Elizabeth Welles. She's here from New England for a little while and we're trying to woo her to relocate permanently. Elizabeth, this is my friend Deena, Jane who owns this lovely home, and Crystal, consummate soccer mom, but looks like a model."

"Hi, glad to meet you," Elizabeth replied, her confidence waning. "I'd forgotten how beautiful the summer nights are here. Perfect for pool parties." Small talk was painful for Elizabeth. She felt that familiar tug to retreat into herself.

"Welcome to the southland. Hope you'll feel at home here. I know Jenna would love it. You're from the Boston area? How ever did you get there from here?" Crystal, a diminutive blonde with upswept hair wearing a bold red dress, asked with an enchanting smile exposing her perfect teeth.

"It's complicated, but then isn't everything? Actually, I'd always wanted to live there and went to school and stayed." Elizabeth offered a lighter version of her reasons.

"Tell us more about you, dear. Looks as if you have been enjoying some sun." Jane White kindly assessed Elizabeth.

"I'm an architectural illustrator specializing in industrial complexes. That's about all there is to tell."

"She's way too modest. She not only creates magic with AutoCad, but is an extraordinary artist. Her hand renderings are gorgeous," Jenna said.

"I love historic architecture. Your home would be a fantastic subject, Jane." Elizabeth said to her host.

"Perhaps we can arrange a commission," she smiled and took Elizabeth's arm. "I'm going to steal your sister-in-law and get her a plate and we'll circulate," Jane said, as they took leave of the other three.

Jane White exuded class and everything proper. Elizabeth felt comfortable, welcomed and at ease with the matriarch. She introduced Elizabeth to various people, as they walked along poolside to a food tent. Doug was there filling his plate with succulent slices of ham and sampled every salad bowl with a scoop from each.

"Sister! I see you're in good hands—Jane is the quintessential hostess," he nodded toward her.

"She is! You have an impressive ensemble of colleagues, Doug. I'm so proud of you!"

"I'll leave you two and catch up later. We have that commission to discuss, Elizabeth," Jane said smiling as her elegant form disappeared among the people gathered underneath the tent.

"Take a plate—then come sit with me over there," he motioned toward a wicker ensemble of outdoor furniture on the patio.

Elizabeth selected mainly salads, but not without adding a couple of tempura shrimp. The siblings claimed the spot Doug pointed out.

"Would you like another wine? Pinot Gris?" he asked.

Elizabeth nodded, placed her napkin on her lap and waited for him to return. As she sampled a bite of food, she was aware that someone came through the doors behind her, and before she could turn around, a leathery, European scent preceded the man of about forty who appeared in front of her. After she got past his wavy hair and tan that showcased the palest blue eyes she had ever seen, she observed he was dressed impeccably casual in beige slacks, white shirt and Italian loafers. Expensive ones.

Looking at Doug's plate on the round coffee table he said, "I see you have company?" May I join you?" He sat without her saying yes, but she didn't mind. "I'm Anthony Dearborn. And you are?"

Elizabeth was mesmerized at his sophistication and élan and could hardly find her voice. "Elizabeth Welles. I'm Doug Potter's sister." She felt awkward and wished her brother would return and she searched the crowd around the bar.

"It's a lovely night for such an event, don't you think? Do you live nearby or . . . ? I didn't know Doug had such a beautiful sister. Where has he been hiding you?"

His eyes disarmed every part of her. Not just his eyes, his whole being. She felt a hot blood rise to her cheeks and was grateful for the subdued lighting.

Doug ambled up to the table. "Tony, I see you've met Elizabeth. Please join us," he said, and handed the wine glass to his sister, then sat in a cushy wicker chair.

Anthony rose to his full height of at least six feet. "I will find you later—looks like this is my cue to mingle," then turned to Elizabeth. "So very nice to meet you. We shall not be strangers." He smiled and smoothly exited.

Elizabeth detected an accent, making Anthony Dearborn all that more attractive. "Oh my God, Doug, who on earth is that man? I could hardly find my tongue," she waved her hand in front of her face like a fan to feign cooling off.

"Tony's our European connection. Major asset. Unattached, I might add, but his travels would not enhance a relationship," Doug said. "Are you interested? He looked interested in you," he grinned, as he took a hearty bite.

"He's from another world, Doug. Sort of like Stephen's sister who lives abroad. Their echelon is not included in any of my fantasies, but it doesn't hurt to enjoy the moment." She sampled her wine. "Mmm, very nice," she said, as she watched Anthony maneuver ever-so-elegantly through the crowds.

"I'm amazed how far you've come this past year, Liz. I'm also grateful. Don't sell yourself short. Tony's a catch and he's obviously intrigued. Who am I to say? He handles all the international banking aspects when real estate and trusts are involved. He's based in Switzerland. The consortium has allowed us to expand outside the states."

"I really am proud of your accomplishments, Doug, but not surprised. Always knew you'd be mega-successful. Thanks for the introduction into your circuit, but it's so foreign to me," she squeezed her brother's arm.

"I know it's only been a few days. Are you warming up to Southern California yet?" Doug asked.

"It just got a lot warmer," she said, as she refocused her gaze on Anthony.

Doug followed her line of sight and smiled. "Could be interesting to keep it all in the family."

Elizabeth circulated throughout the evening with either Jenna or Doug beside her, and was more animated than when she arrived, relaxed by dinner and more than two glasses of Pinot. She and Jenna met up with Jane who insisted on giving them a guided tour of the imposing home with its eight bedrooms, sitting rooms and gourmet kitchen just like one you would find in a Tuscan villa with copper pots and pans suspended over a massive cooktop. A built-in brick oven awed Elizabeth. The bones of this mansion were lovely, indeed.

"What do you think about something 24"x36" with a classic double matte and gilded frame?" she asked Elizabeth at their last stop in the foyer. "I can move that mirror and that wall space would be perfect for it," her enthusiasm was palpable.

"I might suggest matching the size of the mirror," Liz responded. "I'd like to take some photos in daylight of the exterior—maybe this week-end?" she looked at Jenna then back to Jane. "I'm going home next Friday, so . . ."

"Anytime, just let me know and we'll have the gates open," Jane clasped her hands and looked at the space where Elizabeth's rendering would hang.

"Channing has soccer tomorrow, but maybe after the game," Jenna said. "Will that work, Liz?"

Elizabeth nodded. "Could we measure the mirror?"

"I think there's a tape measure in the kitchen in one of those messy drawers we all have," she joked, and left the room.

"I'm glad I didn't hang out in the den," Liz jabbed Jenna's arm.

"I'm going to round up Doug. We need to get going pretty soon. We'll find you. Super exciting to get a job out of this! Way to go, Liz!" She turned and went through a columned archway toward the pool area.

Jane returned with a scale that was almost the size of her hand and something to write with. "This ought to do it."

"And then some," Liz said, as she pulled the metal tape from its casing. She recorded the measurements on the sticky note pad that Jane had brought and pulled off a sheet.

"Thank you, Jane, I certainly never expected . . ." Liz murmured humbly.

Jane looked at her squarely. "Neither did I." She grasped Elizabeth's elbow and steered her toward the kitchen which was cluttered with food and dishes and glassware that was being attended to by a small staff of caterers. "You go ahead. I need to give a little direction here."

Elizabeth continued on to the pool area, moving with the music as she went.

Anthony Dearborn was waiting for her as she parted the glass doors and stepped out onto the patio. "Elizabeth," he said with velvet and gravel in his voice.

She was embarrassed that he caught her dancing by herself like a teen. "Oh, hi, I was just looking for Jenna. I think we're ready to call it an evening."

"That's a shame. It's just getting started. In Swisse we eat dinner later and take it slower," he moved into her personal space and every defense drained out of her.

"Hey, Liz," Jenna approached the couple in the shadows. "Doug's coming along shortly, do you want to say good-bye to the Whites and . . ." she quickly summed up how silly that sounded. Liz was not a little girl. "I need to get up with Channing tomorrow for her game and you wanted to return to take photos . . ."

Anthony stepped forward ever so slightly into Jenna's space. "That's a pity. Elizabeth and I were just starting to get to know one another. Maybe you could cut her loose and I could take her home?" Anthony asked with what could have been a flirty wink to Jenna.

"I, uh, well, are you ok with that, Liz?" Jenna looked for a clue in Elizabeth's expression.

"Don't depend on me for directions. Do I need a key?" Elizabeth had a sparkle in her eye.

"I'll leave the kitchen side door open." Jenna offered as a solution.

Doug approached them. "Tony. Looks like you snagged the two prettiest women here." He hugged them both.

"Anthony's going to take Liz home." Jenna said.

"Great, then." Doug's gaze locked on Liz. "We'll see you later. Take care of her, my man," and shook Tony's hand.

The couple departed leaving Elizabeth and Anthony standing in the soft light.

Chapter Thirty-Two

In the Cross-Hairs of Fate

The breakfast bar was crowded with juice, milk and several cereal choices and mismatched coffee mugs and bowls. "Well, he offered, and that way you won't have to be pressured getting back from the soccer game to pick me up," Elizabeth said to Jenna, as she poured milk over her cereal. "You know what they say about house guests after three days . . ." she smiled and shoved a spoonful of granola into her mouth.

"Don't be silly, we're family," Jenna said, dumping a chopped banana into the blender. "Seems like you and Anthony clicked. Are you and Alek over, if you don't mind me asking?"

"You've got to admit he's easy on the eyes." Elizabeth grinned at her sister-in-law who nodded an assent. "Alek and I both decided to take a break. I miss him, but with his decision to accept the job offer in Germany, I'm not on board. Just not up for a long-distance relationship. He really wants me to go with him, but I've had enough upheaval and need to find that place called home and Germany isn't it."

"Sounds like you've got a good handle on it, and it's not been that long, but sometimes opportunity comes along and you don't even see it. Just don't overthink it, Liz." Jenna whirred the blender and poured her smoothie into a portable insulated container.

Her words shifted Elizabeth's mood.

"I'll keep that in mind. Meanwhile, I have a date." Elizabeth was a little giddy. "Gotta get ready. See you later and enjoy your run and game today."

"Life in the fast lane, remember?"

Jenna and Elizabeth loved to spar. They were more like sisters.

"I'll wear my track shoes."

※ ※ ※

A black Porsche convertible, top down, rolled in the driveway. The cloudless day and brilliant sunshine warranted it. Anthony wore crisp powder-blue Bermuda shorts, the color of his eyes, and a white polo shirt that showed off his magnificent olive skin deepened by the sun. He could be a fashion model.

Elizabeth answered the door, ready for the day. She made a slight gasp and wondered if she was having a surreal experience or if the angels were playing with her. She glanced at the shiny vehicle with its top down and was grateful she had a hat and wore her hair back.

"Good morning. All ready," she smiled broadly, as she slung the strap of her burlap tote onto her shoulder.

"Great. Hope you don't mind the top down. It is such a gorgeous day, I hated to waste it." Anthony laced her arm through his and squeezed her hand, as he led her to the car and opened her door.

"It's really nice of you to take me back to the White's today. Morning shots of their villa should be a perfect blend of light and shadow," Liz said, adjusting her seat belt, hat and dark glasses. She sneaked a sideways peek at Anthony, as he started the car. His profile was stellar. The artist in her loved his sharp features and mature look. The woman in her was smitten.

"It's my pleasure. If you don't have plans afterward, I know a magical little bistro in Santa Monica with cuisine surpassing any I have had in L.A. Are you game?" He accelerated smoothly and turned onto the street.

"I'm game."

The restaurant was crowded, but Anthony spoke to the hostess and Elizabeth could not believe how the waters parted for him. She had not experienced this type of relationship before. Anthony was continental to the nth and subtly knew how to put her at ease when she felt awkward. There were times when she sensed Sandalphon and Metatron watching her, prompting her or she may have been remembering them from a dream. A woman with heavy bangs and raven black hair straight to her hips escorted them to a corner in the back of the restaurant. It was an intimate space perfect for sharing food and conversation.

"Two Bellinis," he said to the woman, as he handed Elizabeth a menu.

"Is there a specialty you'd recommend?" Liz asked, taking in the ambiance and deciding to let him be in control.

He looked up from the menu straight into her eyes and she felt a spark somewhere, everywhere.

"I suggest the glazed salmon. Pure heaven."

Elizabeth noticed her hands were shaking as she held the menu so she laid it down on the table. "Perfect."

"Let's take a look at your photo shoot. Something tells me you have a superb artist's eye and captured all the right details."

Elizabeth retrieved her phone from her bag and pulled up the images of the Renaissance villa. "It was so imposing, it was hard to get the angles and light just right," she said, as she scrolled through the frames. "Here, this one's pretty good," and handed the phone to him. She could not believe the electrical charge she felt when their fingers grazed each other.

"Yes, it will make an astonishing piece of art. Pity you cannot stay long enough to complete it here for Jane," he said, as the server delivered the pastel bubbly in delicate crystal flutes that resembled Greek columns. He handed one to Elizabeth and the bubbles tickled her nose as she took the first sip.

૨૭ ૨૭ ૨૭

The black Porsche snaked its way up the coast toward Malibu along windy roads past rocky cliffs. Elizabeth held her face toward the cool ocean air and peeked at the sunset that was beginning to blossom on the horizon spilling multiple shades of pink and orange into the ethers. Despite the sunscreen and hat, unused to this much sun, Elizabeth's face and shoulders were glowing.

"At home they call this 'the pink moment,' meaning it's cocktail time," Elizabeth said, after a long stretch of silence.

"Shall we stop and take advantage of your tradition?" Anthony asked, without looking at her. "My place is just a few miles farther."

Elizabeth's heart skipped. "You didn't mention you had a place here as well as Geneva." She drew herself in, pulled her pashmina from her bag in the seat back, feeling suddenly chilled. "I should be getting home. It's been an awesome day, but I don't know what Doug and Jenna had planned, and . . ."

"Why don't you give them a call. Besides, we can't waste the pink moment," his delivery was smooth which made Elizabeth uncomfortable. Her instincts were screaming.

She selected Jenna's number from her contact list and punched it in. She learned that the kids had requested hot dogs for dinner. Jenna giggled, told her to go for it, and that they would leave the light on, but wouldn't wait up. "Looks like they won't miss me." Elizabeth caught his smile in the mirror.

The views were indescribable. A panorama of a hundred and eighty degrees was visible through ceiling-to-floor twenty-foot windows that wrapped around the entire front of the house and literally made Elizabeth dizzy and almost speechless. A circular flagstone fireplace in the center of the great room extended up to the vaulted ceiling and dominated the space. Über-sleek modern furniture punctuated several areas around the fireplace and in front of the window. On one end of the expansive great room was a stainless industrial kitchen and a massive island with a slab of sparkly white quartz on top that looked as if it had never been used. On the opposite end of the room was a ship's bow-shaped extension of windows where the grand piano was showcased on a slightly raised platform.

"Do you spend much time here? That view, this room, it's stunning, Anthony." Elizabeth found her voice and finally commented on the obvious.

"Thank you. Unfortunately, I do not. Geneva is my home, but I am here several times a year and I like having something to call my own," he said, as he went to the stainless fridge, scanned the contents and selected a wheel of cheese and set it on the island. "What does a pink moment call for?"

Elizabeth, who was mesmerized by the view and the growing silvery reflections from the sun on the water, turned toward Anthony.

"Usually a mixed drink or Scotch or rye—pretty old school."

"I'll surprise you."

He busied himself in a cabinet and found crackers and a marble slab for the cheese.

Elizabeth wondered how she found herself in this situation and where it was going. It was ridiculous to think he could be interested in someone as unworldly as she was, and decided her brother must have set this up to make her feel comfortable and sweeten the pot to make her move here.

Anthony deftly handled a metallic shaker adding ice and Grey Goose and a hint of vermouth and extracted two almond-stuffed green olives from a jar. He was perfection to watch and knew how to treat a woman, so she decided to take the advice of one of her professors when he described reading the prescribed textbook for the course. "If it's inevitable, you might as well lay back and enjoy it."

Elizabeth brought the appetizers to a glass-topped side table by the leather couch, sat and waited for Anthony to bring the martinis. He flipped the switch on the gas fireplace and sat next to her and they were toasting once again. The sky glowed as he placed his arm around the back of the couch drawing closer to Elizabeth. Her thoughts raced and her cheeks burned, but this moment may never come again, so she embraced her professor's words and let herself be kissed.

Chapter Thirty-Three

Betwixt and Between

Elizabeth dumped a stack of mail onto her desk. She set the summer chic straw bag she purchased before she left next to the pile and extracted her phone from it. The one-bedroom condo she had rented near the City Center of New Bristol was adequate and functional, but had temporary written all over it. It felt strange returning to a place where she had no history and it made her miss her family. Most of her belongings were in storage because she rented this unit month-to-month on the fly with the intention of finding something permanent when she had more time. Outside of a few keepsakes, her computer equipment and paintings, it did not feel inviting, much less like home. Doubts crept in and out. She missed her house and questioned whether she did the right thing selling it, but the inevitable conclusion was a fresh start without associations was a healthy logical choice.

She punched in a number and waited for her friend to pick up. "Hey, Marni. I just got in. Jet-lagged, but not bad." Elizabeth sat on the arm of the beige sofa that came with the place and kicked off her shoes. "Have the bridesmaid dresses come in yet? It's getting close, Marn," she said, as she jumped up to adjust the a/c and peeled off her light cardigan. "This week? Sure, I can do a fitting, but I need a couple of days to settle in. I'll get back to you and we'll catch up. Maybe we could take a drive to the shore."

Marni detected her friend's tone was lighter.

"Something's up, I can feel it. Have you talked with Alek?" Marni asked.

Elizabeth shrugged her shoulders and opened the fridge and grabbed a bottle of water. "We spoke a few times, but honestly, Doug and Jenna kept me so busy and . . ."

"I knew it. You've met someone," Marni's voice rose in excitement.

"I met lots of people," Elizabeth said coyly, untwisting the bottle cap. "It'll have to keep. As they say in L.A., 'it's complicated.'"

☙ ☙ ☙

Elizabeth stood in front of a closet crowded with too many clothes and squeezed in the white blazer she took with her, but never wore, then went back to the bed and zipped her suitcase shut. She checked on her bath water and found the tub almost filled and was ready for a deep soak. She sprinkled lavender bath crystals under the spigot and swished the water, blending them in. Embracing the quiet of the small living space and the solitude it provided came easy for her, and after the long flight and hours of processing her recent experiences, conversations and options she faced, she was ready to escape to a place of abandon and the healing it afforded her. Clarity lay waiting to surface in the lavender-scented bath water. She tested the temperature, added a little more from the hot water spigot and gingerly climbed in.

Shadows fell across the courtyard in angular slants that transformed the gardens into a green geometric collage. Elizabeth, in a mint-green terry cover-up, stared out the picture windows which she considered to be the best feature when she viewed the property. A glass of iced tea sweated moisture onto a woven coaster on the side table. Her phone buzzed in her pocket.

"Doug. Sorry I didn't let you know I got in ok. Yeah, the trip went fine, but the hermit in me wanted to get home and soak in a tub—sorta straightens out all the kinks. How's it going there? I can't believe I'm here," she reflected on her words then added, "I mean, it's surreal to think that in a few hours you can go from one end of the country to another."

"We loved having you, Liz. We miss you already. The time went too fast. Everyone enjoyed getting to know you, some more than others," Doug needled his sister. "The kids are pesky asking when Aunt Liz is coming back."

"Give 'em special hugs from me. I'll bet Jenna will be glad to get back to her routine. It was generous of her to put her Pilates classes in the hands of someone else for a few weeks. You, too, although I suspect your laptop got a workout after hours," she said.

"I told Jenna we wouldn't get away with it. But seriously, we want you to come back. Permanently, and I know it wouldn't break Anthony's heart if you did."

She paused before responding to avoid taking the bait. "Sitting on that fence is not a comfortable place to be with all those pointy pickets, but whatever I decide has to be right. I'm getting closer. Flying into Boston and seeing that familiar skyline and bay definitely warmed a few cockles in my heart." Elizabeth stood and stretched and padded barefoot to the windows. "You'll be the first to know when I sort this out, but in the meantime, I'm super busy with Marni's wedding and I need to get a new contract going—there are a few projects I want to bid on—and there's the White's commission. That was so gracious of her," Elizabeth's voice was wistful. "I have loose ends everywhere, but it's ok. My whirlwind L.A. fantasy will have to sustain me throughout it all. Thank you for everything, dear brother. I can't believe how lucky we are."

"Neither can I, Liz. I love that something good came out of something tragic."

Elizabeth's eyes filled with moisture and she nodded imperceptibly into the phone.

The breakfast bar was a perfect place to eat supper while sorting the mail with the evening news providing white noise in the background. She cobbled together a dinner of Mrs. Stouffer's lasagna and the last of a bag of frozen spinach and vowed tomorrow would include serious grocery shopping. She tossed bills, junk mail and unknowns into three piles and was surprised to see an envelope from her own stationery collection pop up in the mix. The finely scripted hand spelling out her name and former location (it had been forwarded to her current address) seemed familiar, and the return address on the back indicated a note from Sister Antoinette. She set it aside and would open it later because Antoinette had a way of seeing through her and Elizabeth didn't want to be that visible right now. With her heart rate elevated a little, she slid off the stool at the counter and searched the pantry and found a package of stale vanilla cookies which she was about to open when the doorbell rang. She set the box on the counter and peeped through the security lens in the door and saw a massive burst of color. She opened the door and a delivery person stood there extending a cut crystal vase with enormous orange and pink star lilies, sunset-colored roses and luscious greenery.

"Ms. Elizabeth Welles?" the young man asked.

"Yes. Who on earth? They're lovely! Thank you," she said, as she accepted the arrangement and closed the door.

Her pulse sped up as she plucked the card from the holder in the center of the bouquet. She opened it and read: "Hopefully, this arrives at a pink moment. I will treasure our time and think of you at sunset. Love, Anthony."

Elizabeth drank in the freshness of the flowers and laid the card beside the exquisite vase. This wasn't going to be easy and felt herself on that fence again.

Chapter Thirty-Four

Transformation

After a day of phone calls, paperwork, errands and appreciative glances at her sunset bouquet, Elizabeth resolved to open Sister Antoinette's note. The nun remained an enigma and Elizabeth was not entirely comfortable with that. She suspected Sister Antoinette for whatever reason continued to need her to validate what happens after death and substantiate that the ancient texts that told of The Watchers were authentic.

The rendering on the note card reminded her she was content doing what she did professionally; she linked that thought with translating the photos of the faux Italian estate into a full-blown rendering. Her mind drifted back to the evening at the White's where fate arranged for her to meet Anthony. It was dream-like and confusing all at the same time.

Her cell phone buzzed on top of a stack of work proposals on her desk. She recognized the number. "Alek. Hi," she said, as she eyed the lovely blooms perched on the parson's table in her entry way.

"Elizabeth. When did you get in? How was your trip?" Alek asked a stream of questions.

"Yesterday, afternoon. Trying to get it together today working my checklist," she sat back and picked up a mechanical pencil and doodled on a personalized notepad that read, "From the desk of . . ." "I had a great time, but it's an intense scene. It's good to be back, but loved being with my family," an awkward few beats of dead air passed.

"I thought you might like to get together, grab a bite or whatever sounds good, and we can catch up," Alek offered.

"Sure, I'd like that. Will 7:00 work?" Elizabeth monitored her voice and realized it lacked warmth and enthusiasm, and tried to be brighter. "How about Giavonni's?" she suggested.

"Perfect. See you soon," he said.

Elizabeth terminated the call and pocketed the phone, as she walked to the alcove by her bedroom. Her stackable washer and dryer had been humming on and off all day and she took out the last load of items still warm from their tumble and held them to her chest. She picked out the light cotton apple-red peasant blouse with embroidered flowers to wear over white skinny jeans, then folded and put the other garments into the closet and drawers. She stepped into the shower and lost herself in the healing warmth of the water.

She was refreshed after she dried her hair and applied light make-up. She approved of the woman looking back at her in the bathroom mirror, and noticed her tanned skin enhanced her looks. She glowed. Elizabeth had laid her outfit on the bed and when she reached for the red blouse, a sleepiness overcame her which she could not resist. Her eyelids were leaden and she fell onto the bed before the dream overtook her.

A portal of rubies arched over her head and she passed under them gliding easily into the land beyond where her angels, Metatron and Sandalphon waited, eyes fastened on hers with intensity and seriousness. Sandalphon had a white satin cape draped over his arm and met her on the silvery pathway that extended to the horizon and their world. Metatron moved like smoke toward Elizabeth and the three beings traveled the road until they disappeared in the shimmering distance.

Time did not exist in this realm and movement was easy. Elizabeth could not tell if their journey had taken an hour or a minute when they came upon an altar at the edge of a vast precipice. The altar was chiseled out of white marble revealing ornate carvings and adorned with glistening rubies and pearls. Elizabeth edged toward the side of the chasm and saw there was no bottom, no earth beneath only endless space. Sandalphon lightly spread the cloak over the altar, its whiteness blending with the marble.

Metatron uttered in his most melodic voice, "You are here because that which is written is about to unfold," he stared and their gazes locked. A little fear and great love engulfed her. "We have broadened your world to move you closer to fulfilling your destiny."

Elizabeth studied the way her mentor moved around her and the altar as he spoke. She dared to glance over the side of the cliff again and felt a tingle wondering if they were about to sacrifice her and then was astonished at her insane thoughts. That was the old Elizabeth's mentality. A wave of gratitude washed over her, knowing she had chosen to follow the guidance and wisdom of these Divine beings.

Sandalphon rested his hand like a butterfly on her shoulder. "Your purpose is on the brink of being fulfilled." He swirled around her and yet never broke their connection. "After your initiation, you will be changed at depth and will have clarity about your path and direction." Sandalphon reverently lifted the garment off the altar. Each angel held up a side of the ceremonial cape in front of the marble slab framed by an endless cerulean blue sky.

Elizabeth was solemn and ready to embrace whatever happened. She surrendered whatever fear was tucked into the nether regions of her mind and heart while an image of Stephen flooded her mind in waves of light. She stepped between the two archangels who had shepherded her soul to this point looking into Metatron's glistening black eyes and the heavenly blue of Sandalphon's. She absorbed an outpouring of great love and in its flow observed pictures and scenes of her future life that flashed like a movie in her head as the white cloak was solemnly placed on her shoulders. Her entire being was awash in white light. She turned and stood with her companions facing the edge of the precipice and she was infused with the enormity of space and time and dimension. Elizabeth became one with all that is or was or ever will be. And it was done.

Elizabeth's eyes shot open and she was aware of being on her back on her bed with the doorbell ringing insistently. She quickly dressed and called out to Alek, noticing the clock said 7:05, as she ran past it on her nightstand.

Breathless, she yanked the door open and Alek stood in the hallway looking concerned. He stepped over the threshold without being asked and embraced and kissed her lightly before she pulled away. "You okay?" He studied Elizabeth as he moved into her personal space.

"I must have been more jet-lagged than I thought. I, uh, fell asleep after my shower and the doorbell woke me up," she said, checking her hair in the hall mirror. She completely forgot about the flowers on the table.

Alek eyed the bouquet. "Looks like you have an admirer," he said.

"Yes, well . . ." she pulled him by the hand to the front room where he sat down on the beige couch. "Would you like anything before we leave?" Nervously she backed up toward the kitchen adjusting the ties on her blouse.

"No, I'm fine—it's just great to see you, uh, looking so well. That California sun agreed with you," he said, as he appraised her approvingly.

Elizabeth flashed a smile when she exited the room.

Alek had never seen her smile like that before which put him ill-at-ease with this woman who could end up being his fiancé.

❧ ❧ ❧

The restaurant had cleared except for a few customers who huddled over their Chianti and nibbled breadsticks. Elizabeth and Alek sat side-by-side, both drinking coffee, in a booth with a checkered cloth and a votive candle that flickered in its last stage of life. Elizabeth looked up as the server came by with a pot to give her a fill, but she waived him off.

"You know I couldn't pass up the opportunity, Liz." His voice was low, but earnest. "Please reconsider." His eyes melted her heart and his sincerity was genuine. "We could make it work."

She shook her head, looking down, avoiding his gaze. "I can't explain it. I just know we would both regret 'making it work.' You need to trust me, Alek. I'm clear about what my life is supposed to look like and relocating to Germany isn't part of it."

"Is it 'Mr. Star Lilies'? he asked, pulling his hands away from hers, sitting upright.

"He's Doug's business associate." Elizabeth omitted the details of their mutual attraction.

An uncomfortable silence dragged on before Elizabeth put her napkin on the table and scooted down to the end of the booth. Without uttering a word, Alek followed and paused to drape her sweater over her shoulders before they exited the restaurant. It reminded Elizabeth of the powerful moment when those angelic beings endowed her with the silvery white cloak.

Elizabeth focused her vision straight ahead, as Alek pulled into a visitor's parking space in the condo units and turned off the engine. The couple exchanged a few words of polite conversation on the drive to Elizabeth's. Now the inevitable awkward moment stood between them like a cement wall.

"We both know what we have has been the best and I don't regret one moment. You were there for me when no one else was. I couldn't have gotten through this past year without you, Alek. I hope you know how grateful I am and always will be," she said, still unable to look at him full-on. "I really am happy you're taking this next step for your career. It would be foolish not to."

"At the expense of losing you," he said quietly.

"The contract's just for a couple of years. Neither of us knows what will happen. Living abroad will open more doors than you can imagine and I'm a little envious, but not too much," she said in a lighter tone with a smile in her eyes. "I just know the timing isn't right for me."

He pulled her close and the hug and kiss was emotional for them both. Elizabeth wiped her face with her sleeve and opened the door; the interior dashboard light revealed a tear glinting off Alek's cheek.

"Stay in touch. I love you, Alek, my knight in shining armor." She blew him a kiss and disappeared around the corner of a well-lit pathway to her door.

Chapter Thirty-Five

Promises

Metallic helium-filled balloons hovered and bounced in the air in Mrs. Petrakis' living room. A bounty of floral arrangements and tables piled with endless finger foods and presents surrounded an enormous cut glass punchbowl with the dregs of ice cream-pink liquid pooling on the bottom. "Congratulations" banners, streamers and swags hung off the chandelier and filled the wall spaces.

"You better learn to cook!" Elizabeth said, as she fingered the stainless cookware set and utensils. "Are you really going to use all this? I expect an invite for homemade crepes before the ink is dry on the marriage certificate," Elizabeth kidded her friend.

"I still say we can make it a double wedding," her friend replied, while gathering up napkins, wads of wrapping paper and ribbon.

"Let's not go there," she replied with a finality in her tone.

Marni ignored her friend and continued to probe. "Are you really that sure, Liz? You and Alek are perfect. What's a little time and distance between lovers?"

Elizabeth was reading the label on a miraculous non-stick skillet and never looked up. "It's a big deal to me. I love Alek, but it has to be right, and his decision made things un-right. That's it."

Marni's reaction at the new Elizabeth left her without a response.

Mrs. Petrakis bolted through the swinging kitchen door with a cardboard box to collect the debris of paper plates and plastic forks and cups.

"You're great, Mom," Marni said, giving her a quick squeeze, as she hustled past her, "but we got this."

"You go. It's your time. Enjoy it for soon you will do the same for your daughter. You'll see." The woman smiled generously at her Marni then turned to Elizabeth. "You, too, Miss Elizabeth. I know these things."

Elizabeth felt tingles and chills which confirmed this wise woman was right.

※ ※ ※

The day of the wedding dawned white hot. Elizabeth could barely breathe and wondered how she would manage the lengthy Greek Orthodox ceremony in the stifling Boston heat. Marni made provisions for each of her guests to receive hand-held mini-electric fans, but her maid of honor and wedding party would have to participate without one. She said a prayer that there would be adequate ventilation in the centuries-old church.

Marni went for the whole experience with a twelve-foot train that Elizabeth was responsible to arrange throughout the day. She was grateful the bridesmaid's dresses were virtually strapless save thin spaghetti straps, but wondered how she'd fare in the full-length chiffon. Elizabeth appreciated the irony that Marni wanted every dress to be a different color so that when her attendants stood on the dais, it would look like a rainbow with red to the outside and purple for the maid of honor. She wondered if the twin archangels had somehow intervened and had a hand in Marni's planning.

Elizabeth draped the garment bag over her arm, pulled up the handle of her carry-on and braved the humid air outside her unit and loaded up her car. She was ready to make the two-hour drive to the hotel where the wedding party gathered. Her GPS took her straight to the high-rise. After checking in, she went to the room she had reserved, as she knew driving home after the reception was not an option. The room was located on the same floor where gaggles of women were primping in adjoining suites and the atmosphere buzzed like a hive from the time she entered.

"Elizabeth!" Marni came running from the bathroom in a pink terry robe, her black curls tamed onto two-inch diameter rollers all over her head. The two friends embraced. "Did you ever think you would see the day?" she asked. "I still can't believe it myself, but Josh is as good as it gets. I knew from day one, but I could never let on." Marni's joy was effervescent.

"You must be a good poker player, Marn. I didn't see it coming, but couldn't be happier for you." They hugged again, and she grabbed Elizabeth by the hand and introduced her to members of her family who were there from out of town. Along the way Elizabeth observed a chain of make-up technicians at work and stylists creating elegant romantic 'dos in every room of the enormous suite.

The women in the wedding party helped each other groom and assisted with every detail to prepare for the main event. The florist delivered the bride's bouquet, white lilies, white roses, baby's breath and sparkling multi-colored jewels poked in between the tightly arranged blooms. Each of the bridesmaid's bouquets matched the color of her dress. Elizabeth's was made up of baby's breath and deep lavender roses which exuded a delicious scent, reminding her of the angelic connection.

Elizabeth laid her bouquet back into its box and helped her friend secure her veil. It was a fingertip creation edged with crystals that framed Marni's upswept black hair with its cluster of dainty curls on one shoulder perfectly.

"You look beautiful, Marni. Josh is going to lose it when he sees you. Are you ready for this?" Elizabeth asked, admiring the Mediterranean beauty before her.

"Since I was a little kid, I pictured this day. I wish the same for you," Marni pulled a white embroidered hanky from the concealed pocket of her ball gown and dabbed her eyes.

"None of that now, you'll ruin your make-up. No raccoon eyes on your wedding day!" Elizabeth attempted to lighten the moment and the women laughed. About that time a large woman in her sixties wearing a short gray lace dress and frothy hat announced that the limo was at the curb. She took charge and shooed everyone in the wedding party out the door to a waiting elevator.

The groom and his attendants gathered in a room off the narthex and the bride and hers assembled in the other chamber. The organ music had been playing light classical arrangements as the guests took their seats. It was only fifteen minutes past the official start time when Elizabeth heard the processional for the bridesmaids and groomsmen start. She hooked arms with Josh's younger brother as they were slated to walk down the aisle first. Elizabeth was clammy from the close quarters and rising temperatures and a mixture of grief and joy. She had scheduled a couple of tune-up sessions with Peter Candless, her counselor at St. John's, in anticipation of meeting strong emotions head-on today. His guidance suggested she concentrate on her friend's happiness and the tried and true, "stay in the moment" routine. Elizabeth was willing to do anything for Marni—she owed her the world.

As the bridesmaids formed their rainbow of color standing on the dais, and the parents and guests were ushered in and seated, the music stopped. After a few moments of silence, the double doors at the rear of the church reopened to reveal a radiant Marni and her dad standing arm-in-arm. When the organ struck the first chords of the wedding march, their vibrations were visceral and the family and guests stood to catch a glimpse of the bride whose magnificent regal ball gown rustled and sparkled down the aisle. Elizabeth watched her friend approach and her throat tightened with awe. She remembered to breathe as flashes of the future sliced through her mind, and she saw herself coming toward her as a bride. Blinking awake into the present, she glanced at Josh to anchor her, and saw his eyes locked on Marni—both bride and groom glowed with anticipation. Handing her purple roses to the bridesmaid in blue chiffon beside her, Elizabeth spread out Marni's voluminous train and the ceremony began.

૨૦ ૨૦ ૨૦

The crowd thinned to less than half, Marni performed the bouquet toss and the newlyweds left for a hotel at an undisclosed location where they would spend the night before leaving on their honeymoon in the Bahamas. Elizabeth shared a cab with other members of the wedding party and went back to the hotel. She was exhausted from the day and the heat that was finally scrubbed out by cooler breezes from the north.

She slid her hotel key into the slot, opened the door to her air-conditioned room and flopped on the bed letting the refrigerated coolness wash over her.

Her mind replayed the day's events and the strange vision of seeing herself as a bride marching down an aisle. The feeling linked to a fear of the unknown, as she could not make out who was waiting for her at the altar.

Chapter Thirty-Six

Falling Into Place

The fall and winter holidays passed unremarkably. After Marni's wedding, Elizabeth made the decision to give herself at least another year in New Bristol. There was no urgency to relocate, as her little condo was adequate and she was beginning to warm up to the convenience of the lifestyle it afforded and made it cozier by sprucing it up with personal appointments and furniture she pulled out of storage that made it her own. She often reflected that Marni was right about condo life for a single person.

After she informed Doug and Jenna that she wanted to stay at least another year in New Bristol, they were disappointed, but gracious enough to understand. Elizabeth thought they probably knew she was not ready to make such a drastic move to California, but they left their offer open. They consistently extended themselves as a lifeline by staying in frequent contact, assuring her that they were a resource, if she felt like she was slipping down that ravine of depression, as unlikely as it was. Those dark incidents had waned, and Elizabeth knew she gained strength each day.

Fred offered more contract opportunities to stay as busy as she wanted work-wise, and she took him up on them. She was juggling several projects and accumulating valuable experience, as they were more technologically challenging and it was rewarding to figure problems out on her own.

Anthony contacted her now and then. Elizabeth understood it was not serious or ever could be, but she loved being put on a pedestal, even if it was a fairy tale. It was an outrageous diversion when he flew into Boston and they went to dinner or met for drinks between flights. She imagined he was the right bridge at the right time to allow her to feel desired, hopeful and open to the possibilities in life she might never have otherwise imagined.

Elizabeth carried two bulky grocery sacks back to her condo and took note that the daffodils were in bloom and the trees had sprouted small round buds. It was only the first part of March, and they served as harbingers of the world awakening to an early spring. Her thoughts revisited the events of two years ago when Stephen died, and it was hard to fathom how time had blurred the pain and how her life had changed.

She shelved and refrigerated her grocery items then washed the produce in a strainer in the sink. When she heard the phone in her purse play Queen's "We Are the Champions", she turned off the water, wiped her hands on a towel and retrieved her cell. "Hey Marni," she answered, meandering to the couch which now had off-white and brown-colored throw pillows along the back and by each arm. "I'm good, how 'bout you?" Elizabeth heard about the dog needing flea control, the dishwasher breaking and the endless laundry with two people under one roof. "Nothing special, just putting in the hours. I'm trying to clean up my files and the house today. I've been super busy with work and I've let things go, you know how it is."

"Same here, but Josh is more domestic than I realized. Talk about a bonus. He's Mr. Neat so can't complain." Marni continued. "Think you can break away? I love married life, but feel girl time coming on."

Elizabeth looked around the living room and her office and decided she needed to create order out of chaos. It was close to tax season and organizing the data would not happen without her. Stephen used to take care of that arm of the household. "Maybe tomorrow? I really need to get things together here."

"Okay, brunch? Art museum afterwards? With the buds starting to pop it should be beautiful on the grounds. I just love this time of year," Marni said.

Wistful, Elizabeth replied, "I used to. Maybe I will again, but yeah, brunch sounds great. A reward for hard work," she smiled and returned to the kitchen. "How about 10:30 at Bayside? Love their buffet."

"Haven't been there forever. Cool. I'll let you go and we'll catch up tomorrow. Love ya."

Tethered to her desk, Elizabeth plied her computer sorting out information, spreadsheets and cleaning up files. She needed to purge in order to organize the newer data. She finished with her work-related files and took a break before she started on the personal pieces she would need for taxes. The sale of her house last year made it more complex than it would have been otherwise; she had not reinvested it into a primary residence so had to deal with that bag of unfamiliar worms after she had her coffee. She had purchased a single drip brewer that made one cup and found herself drinking more of it.

She poured steaming water through the filter and into a mug and the aroma alone revived her. A new bottle of French vanilla creamer was in the fridge and she added a healthy measure after discarding the filter apparatus and took it and her phone to the living room. She positioned herself in front of the windows that brought in beautiful light and views. After a few hearty sips, she decided to purge her phone data to lighten its storage load. She eliminated several apps and old text and email messages that reminded her of the trauma of the past. Peter would be proud of symbolically letting go of that which no longer served her. She checked her contact list and came across Dehlia Townsend's name. Somehow with the fervor of the wedding, the California residue, her workload and shift in her lifestyle, Elizabeth forgot that she had promised to call Dehlia. It was almost a year since they met, and she toyed with the idea whether she needed to honor a commitment with a total stranger she had met on a plane. It would have been easy to press the delete button, but her intuition and ingrained ethics prevailed and she pressed the "call" button instead.

The phone rang more than four times and she was about to hang up when a voice answered out of breath. "Hello?"

"Dehlia Townsend? You may not remember me, but we met on a flight to L.A. last June. I found your number and realized I hadn't stayed in touch, so . . ." Elizabeth felt finding her words awkward.

After a moment, Dehlia responded, "Of course I remember. Are you still in New Bristol?" she asked. "You hadn't made up your mind about California. Did you have a good visit?"

"I'm still here—the trip was great and loved the family time." Elizabeth elaborated a little further, then related the strange coincidence of meeting

Dehlia's daughter Nicole at the beach.

"Nicole mentioned something about it." Dehlia let her voice trail off into silence which added to Elizabeth's discomfort, but then she perked up. "I have a tea room off the sun porch. It's quite nice any time of year, but with everything starting to green up, I think you'd like it."

Elizabeth was reluctant to accept. She could always stave off the inevitable, but her reawakened intuition niggled her. "I'm sure I would."

What about Saturday after next? The azaleas should be in full bloom since everything's showing up earlier this year."

Elizabeth pulled up her calendar app, but did not really need to check. She was not dating and most of her friends were married, so Saturdays were usually the longest days of the week. She accepted and jotted Mrs. Townsend's address and directions on a sticky note. She had forgotten that the township of Gilbert was less than a few hours away.

≥ ≥ ≥

Marni looked fabulous. Even though she was always on the fleshier side, it looked like she had added a couple of pounds, but it agreed with her. It was the glow that made the difference. She and Elizabeth strolled through the rooms that displayed Renaissance paintings commenting on the opulence of the era and the lush details of each masterpiece. Elizabeth's art background allowed her to point out the magic of perspective which was a closely guarded secret of the Italians whereas the oils and their layered applications of pigment created the jewel-tones in the Netherlandish paintings and they guarded their secrets as effectively. The two women took a seat on a velvet-tufted bench across from Giorgione's *The Tempest* and studied it without a word, letting themselves get lost in the allegory of the work.

"This has nothing to do with the painting, but do you remember me telling you about that lady I sat next to on a plane and meeting her daughter when Jenna and the kids and I went to the beach the next day?" Elizabeth asked.

Marni nodded turning to her friend. "And so?"

"When I was cleaning up files yesterday, I ran across her number and actually called her. Something told me I needed do what I'd promised. She invited me to tea."

Marni scrutinized her friend's face carefully. "You really take this coincidence stuff seriously, don't you? So when are you going?"

"In a couple of weeks. Gilbert is closer than I'd remembered." Elizabeth returned her attention to the painting. She wanted to tell her friend more about the world that had opened up to her, but Marni remained only quasi-receptive and this did not seem like the right time to delve into that part of her life.

"I feel like the Renaissance is getting too heavy and closing in. Let's find the Impressionists. Think we can get near that special exhibit of Mary Cassatt's art? If we don't catch it today, it's on display through the end of the month." Marni rose and Elizabeth checked her brochure to find where the exhibit was located.

There were hoards queued up, but the two fell into line and eventually filed into a small room with ink blue walls and exquisite lighting that featured dozens of Cassatt's artwork. The mother and child theme was pervasive and tender and both Marni and Elizabeth commented how sensitive her work was and how it conveyed that unique bond. Elizabeth thought about her own mother and how she did not live long enough to hold her. Elizabeth always felt never being held in her mother's arms was a vital piece missing from her life. A simple, yet complex component necessary to create a familial relationship.

They were pressed into a line of people passing by each painting commenting on and appreciating the phenomenal aspects of light and perspective that permeated the art. Elizabeth was drawn to *The Bath*, a small humble rendering depicting a mother and child at bath time as it would have been in the Victorian era. Its linear qualities showed an influence of Japanese woodcuts which were incorporated into many of Cassatt's compositions, as well as those of other Impressionists. After they emerged from the exhibit, Marni suggested they find a restroom and the two women went in search of one.

"It must've been tough being a mom in those days," Elizabeth said, "no Pampers, Baby Wipes or washing machines."

"I'm grateful I live now because I'm pregnant," Marni said, dropping the tidbit into the conversation barely able to contain her excitement.

"Oh my God, Marn, that's fantastic! I can't believe it! When are you due? Tell me!"

"I thought you'd get the drift with the mother and child theme, but you'd think I'd learn I can't be subtle with you," Marni teased.

Elizabeth bear-hugged her friend in front of the restroom, happier than she had been in a long, long while.

Chapter Thirty-Seven

Rites of Spring

Dehlia Townsend was right about the early spring. The flowers had a mind of their own pushing out to bloom weeks ahead of schedule. Elizabeth left her condo a little before noon to allow plenty of time to make it by two o'clock for a visit with Dehlia. She planned to stop at a local nursery along the way and pick up a potted plant and enjoy the country scenery. West of the suburbs of New Bristol lay open farmland which became instantly rustic with generational century farms that punctuated the landscape.

She drove by a grange-type of feed store with rusting gas pumps from another era stored on a side of the building that was in dire need of paint. There was a small nursery in the side yard where seedlings and starts were displayed, as they were ready for planting. Elizabeth pulled into the gravel parking area and popped loose from her seatbelt. She entered the nursery area and poked through a section of plants for inspiration. The whitewashed tables with worn oilcloth coverings reminded her of why she loved the traditional flavor of New England.

"Help you find anything, Miss?" a raspy voice behind her inquired.

She turned around to find a portly white-haired man in overalls with dirt smudges on the knees.

"I'm not sure what I want. Perhaps you could suggest something for a hospitality gift?"

"What do they like?"

"I don't know her well. Perhaps you know Dehlia . . ."

". . . Townsend," finishing her sentence. "Going for tea?" He grinned and pointed his index finger to his gray temple that needed a trim. "Follow me."

He tottered down the narrow aisle and turned right where there was more acreage behind a wall with bedding plants galore. He nodded toward a pallet of lilacs. "Couldn't miss with one of these."

The plants appeared healthy with generous clusters of sweet-scented flowers. "What about a pink one?" Elizabeth asked.

"She'd be pleased."

"Pick a good one for me," Elizabeth requested, and he selected one a little taller than the rest that was rich with blooms.

The GPS indicated a quarter of a mile ahead on the right. The lane was lined with old-growth maples and Elizabeth fantasized how gorgeous this would be in fall with the trees ablaze in their fiery glory. A carved wooden sign came into view at the entrance of an imposing drive: "Townsend Farms, 1835."

Elizabeth drove in and straight for the colonial homestead that sprawled before her. Her eyes popped at the layout and outbuildings and orchards which extended as far as she could see. She heard cows mooing in the distance and farm smells that somehow added to the charm. The brilliant green meadows and arbors reminded her of the realms of The Watchers. She imagined Sandalphon and Metatron ushering her up the doorstep.

Shaking loose from her dreamy reflections, she lifted the plant out of the back seat and climbed the steps to the vintage entrance and took hold of the cold brass ring on the lion's head door knocker and rapped.

🌿 🌿 🌿

The parlor was authentic, complete with pocket doors and horsehair settee. Elizabeth could imagine herself the woman of the manor receiving guests in this cozy room with red wallpaper above the white wainscoting. Dehlia was in her element with a complete silver tea service gleaming on a marble table top between them. They sat in a pair of wing-back chairs upholstered in a pastel needlepoint fabric.

Glancing at the walls, coffered ceiling and porcelain figurines, Elizabeth said, "This makes a perfect tea room."

Dehlia poured and handed her the tea in a paper-thin porcelain cup and saucer so delicate, Elizabeth could not hide the chatter it made in her shaky hands.

"My late husband and I used to take time for tea here when we could. I wanted to continue the tradition." Her smile was warm putting Elizabeth at ease. "I recall you had decisions to make last time we met." Unlike the nervous woman Elizabeth encountered on the plane, Dehlia appeared utterly confident in her lovely parlor and easily steered the conversation.

"Good memory," Elizabeth returned her smile. "It was a crazy time. Returning to a place where I grew up, but left twelve years ago, was a stretch." She took a dainty sip of tea. "It was fabulous being with my brother Doug and his family, but I knew when I left I needed more time here in New Bristol before I could seriously consider returning to that lifestyle." She set her cup on the table cautiously, careful not to shatter the china on the marble slab.

"There has never been a question about my home. When I married John, and walked into his family home, I knew I would never leave."

Dehlia looked out the window past the porch. Her son, Colin, was approaching the front entrance.

"I'm glad you will be here a while." Dehlia smiled at her guest.

"After I returned from my brother's, I got caught up with my friend Marni's wedding last summer then took on more design contracts than I should have. But when I was in California I received an actual commission for a rendering from the wife of one of my brother's business partners. I have to say, that didn't feel like work and would love to do more of it, but I have to pay the bills." Elizabeth was a bit wistful and oddly talkative wanting to fill up pauses in the conversation.

"Perhaps there will be more opportunities. There are many historic homesteads in this area that I'm sure would welcome the type of work you do." Dehlia lifted the teapot, which glinted in the afternoon sun streaming through lace curtains making patterns on the floor. "More tea?"

"I really should be going. It's been lovely." Elizabeth placed her linen napkin on the table next to her cup and stood.

"Let me give you a whirlwind tour before you leave. Perhaps next time you can stay longer and I'll show you where I intend to plant that gorgeous lilac. How did you know pink was my favorite color?" Dehlia rose and parted the pocket doors. "Colin!"

Across the foyer, a man was removing his jacket and looked up. "Hey, mom."

"Come here. I want you to meet my new friend. We met on the plane when I went to see your sister last year," she opened the doors all the way and Elizabeth's eyes locked on Colin Townsend.

"Colin, this is Elizabeth Welles, Elizabeth, my son, Colin." The tanned well-built man was obviously no stranger to outdoor work. He had a shock of wavy brown hair and his soft brown eyes were the color of doeskin. His angular features framed the most winning smile Elizabeth had ever seen. He exuded pure charm and his charisma nearly knocked her over.

"Nice to meet you," her throat almost closed she was so self-conscious and feared she was blushing.

"Welcome to Townsend Farms. Has mom given you the grand tour yet?" the pale blue work shirt draped his fit body in all the right places.

"We were just about to . . ." Elizabeth said.

"Why don't you take Elizabeth around? I'll clean up the dishes and meet you back here," Dehlia suggested.

The charge in the air and the light in Colin's eyes were phenomena that Dehlia had not experienced in a long while.

"If you're busy I can, uh, another time," Elizabeth was not making sense. Her head was filled with thoughts of the initiation where in a white robe she accepted her destiny and her angelic companions informed her that her world was about to change. She was chilled and sweating at the same time.

"My pleasure. It's a beautiful day for it."

The afternoon sun cut sharp angles exposing dust motes and pollen suspended in the shafts of light. Elizabeth was only about an inch or two shorter than Colin, but his presence was enormous and it drew her inside his delicious aura. She floated through the arbors and orchards and learned the history of Townsend Farms from its post-Revolutionary origins to the present. It was used as a hospital during the Civil War and fell into ruin during the depression of the 1930s, but Colin's grandfather added dairy cows and sold farm equipment in order to have cash flow to implement the apple crops. John Townsend, Colin's dad, restored the house and barn and expanded the dairy to market specialty cheeses. Colin took over the ownership after his father died six years earlier, and found his international sales background helped with marketing and overall business acumen needed to allow the farm to survive. As a Century Farm it received subsidies which helped.

"I found I like getting my hands dirty. I grew up with it, but couldn't get away fast enough to make my mark, but after years of living in hotels and eating from buffets, it feels right to be home. I appreciate having the history and familiarity," he earnestly searched Elizabeth's eyes with a twinkle that disarmed her.

"Having roots is a big bonus in life. You've done a great job managing all of this. I wouldn't have known where to start. But I guess it's in your DNA?" she smiled sweetly, gently and Colin took her hand and placed her arm through his and starting walking toward the house.

His hand on hers, and her arm next to his sent electric current through her body unlike anything she had ever experienced. It was like her dream, floating above the terraces with Sandalphon and Metatron who avoided her eyes, but deftly communicated that something was happening. When they turned the corner from the arbor, the house came into view and she wanted to stop time and never let go.

Chapter Thirty-Eight

Under Full Moons

The maternity ward in St. John's was filled to capacity when Marni went into labor that fall. Marni's doctors considered performing a C-section due to being three weeks past her due date and the size of the baby, but miraculously the labor started with a vengeance, and Sophia Elizabeth was born under a full harvest moon in mid-October.

"She doesn't look real, Marni. She has your black hair—and those tiny hands—." Elizabeth was in awe, unable to take her eyes off the baby in Marni's arms.

Marni watched Josh passing out cigars in the hall from the vantage point of her hospital bed. "He's turned into a peacock, Liz." She directed her attention to the infant curled in her arms wearing a pale pink cap, balling her fists. Marni tenderly uncurled them. "Isn't she the most beautiful perfect baby you've ever seen?"

"She is." Liz bent down to gather her arms around the two of them and her head felt light. Sophia's cap zoomed into focus in Elizabeth's field of vision and it transformed into the light pink lilacs that had come and gone earlier in the year. Dehlia had planted Elizabeth's gift at the entrance of the arbor at Townsend Farms. Elizabeth was surprised to feel a hot tear escape her eye and fall onto the infant's arm.

"Why are you crying? This is supposed to be a happy occasion." Marni chided her friend.

"It's a happy tear," the two laughed and little Sophia yawned and opened her dark eyes. She could have sworn their gaze connected, as if the infant lasered a message directly into Elizabeth's soul. She brushed it off as newborns weren't supposed to be able to focus.

That night, Elizabeth awoke and kicked off the comforter that had tangled around her legs. It was twilight bright in her bedroom, and she thought maintenance must have left extra outdoor lights on, so got up to investigate. Her massive living room window displayed a mega moon reflecting the fierceness of the sun's light. Her condo was filled with eerie light and it was chilly. She shuffled back to the master bath and yanked the robe off the hook on the back of the door and quickly wrapped it around her. Thoughts of Marni being a mom and seeing her baby moments after the birth had wired her psyche and made sleep impossible.

Plunking a kettle on the stove, Elizabeth deemed hot chocolate with marshmallows could be the only remedy for this type of wakefulness. She pawed through the pantry to find both ingredients and while she waited for the water to boil, she logged in and decided to see who else might be affected by the moon and was awake and posting on social media. She scrolled through new photos of little Sophia with almost minute-to-minute updates which meant Josh was smitten with his daughter. She smiled as the obnoxious whistle pierced the air.

Perched on her chair at her work station, she read a few of her favorite blogs as she drank the comforting hot chocolate thinking she would have to brush her teeth again. Also thinking and wondering if she would ever have what Marni had. She got squarely honest and argued with herself about the fact she liked the predictable routine that life had fallen into—work, an occasional girlfriend movie night and dating, but a world like Marni's seemed like a remote possibility. She would have to come to terms with that.

Feeling warmed and a little sleepy, she closed down her computer and nestled back underneath the cold sheets. She made a mental note to retrieve the electric blanket from the storage bin next time she changed linens. Summer died suddenly, and she hardly noticed.

Elizabeth dreamed she was seated in the tea room at Townsend Farms. Dehlia had set out a bowl of scarlet camellias from her garden floating in water, and Elizabeth stared too long at them and was whisked into the world of The Watchers. She felt sucked into a vacuum tube that passed through the dazzling color bands that made up each dimension. A massive golden disc dangled like a Chinese gong in the indigo sky and Metatron and Sandalphon stood silhouetted against its luminous glow. She approached them as she had done before, gliding with ease and assuming an air of familiarity. She stopped short when she saw a distant figure emerge in a ribbon of white light beyond the moon—was it Stephen? She could not see a face, but could feel the energy and it was growing weak. The figure retreated into the distance and then completely disappeared and the ribbon disintegrated into thousands of tiny white diamonds sparkling and settling onto the tapestry of the midnight blue sky.

Elizabeth realized she wore the white velvet mantel and felt its comforting weight on her shoulders offering soft warmth. She looked into the angelic faces of her companions she had come to know and love and trust and they silently confirmed that this was farewell. They each cupped their hands and opened them revealing a silvery ball of pulsating light hovering above their palms. In unison, they placed their glistening orbs into Elizabeth's heart and she closed her eyes and absorbed a stream of unconditional love whose radiance filled her entire being. When she opened her eyes, her companions were gone and the snooze alarm harangued her senses until she was fully awake.

❧ ❧ ❧

Elizabeth decided on a traditional ecru fisherman's sweater, dark brown jeans and suede boots to wear to the hayride. She was heady after spending time with Sophia and mused about having the experience of holding her own child. The truth about her mother whose life drained out of her before the nurses could clean up her babe and place her in her arms, continued to haunt Elizabeth. She was sad for her mother and for herself and prayed someday the wound would heal.

Colin would be there any minute. It would be dusk by the time they got to Gilbert. With the days shorter and nights cooler, she last-minute-plucked a tan corduroy jacket with a fleece zip-out lining from the closet and draped it on top of her overnight bag waiting in the entry. Dehlia insisted she stay in the guest room, so she and Colin would not have to make a long drive home after the Harvest BBQ and hayride.

❧ ❧ ❧

Gilbert had a longstanding tradition of ushering in the Fall Season by grilling ears of corn, onions, potatoes, steaks and chicken in fire pits at the fairgrounds. Picnic tables with pumpkin and Indian corn centerpieces and colorful cloths whose corners and edges were thumbtacked to the tabletop underneath, offered up a spread prepared by the farmers in the community of vegetables, salads and more apple pies than Elizabeth had ever seen in one place. It was a well-attended event of the locals celebrating a fruitful harvest, but Elizabeth had never heard of it. Gilbert was like that—a sliver of Americana in a time capsule, off the grid, but fully interfaced with the technological world at large for commerce and other necessities of life.

After bellies were full and the sky moved past sunset, a hayride capped the evening. Colin and Elizabeth were crowded in with dozens of others in a wooden cart pulled by two workhorses that snorted and bobbed their heads, anxious to perform their task of pulling the wagon on the trails. Hay bales on the bed of the cart provided seating and insulation from the falling temps. After everyone settled down, the horses set out and meandered through the fields of a farm adjacent to the fairgrounds. The scene was immersed in a wash of pale-orange light from an enormous blood-red harvest moon that rose on the eastern horizon. The photo-op was irresistible and people snapped cameras to capture the numerous views of fields of pumpkins, scarecrows and sunflowers spreading around them. This was the living essence of New England that Elizabeth had longed for and imagined experiencing when she was a little girl. She must have read about it or seen it in a picture book, since she'd never been there. In the magic of the moment, she realized her dream and scrunched closer to Colin. She laid her head on his solid shoulder, and he pulled her closer. They fit together perfectly and the physical charge between them had grown into high voltage electricity during the past few months.

"What's up in that beautiful head of yours?" Colin asked.

"Drinking it all in. I must be on another planet. Did you order that moon, or what?"

The couple turned their faces toward the rising orb. Elizabeth swept her arm to the sky and surrounding farm. "Honestly, this whole thing fulfills a fantasy. I can't say how or why but, er, I can't explain . . ." She turned toward him. "Why did you ever want to leave here, Colin?"

"The important thing is I returned." He lightly touched his mouth to hers.

❧ ❧ ❧

Dehlia set up the breakfast offerings on the island for the morning—coffee pot, mugs, a jar of blackberry jam and a tin-foil-covered plate of scones. She turned out the kitchen light and made her way to the base of the stairs. With one hand on a newel post and a petite foot on the first riser, she turned to the lovers who were headed out to the sunroom with a bottle of wine and an afghan, "Good night you two. I left towels on the bed and an extra blanket on top of the dresser, Elizabeth. Feel free to sleep in—I'm usually puttering before the chickens wake up, so I'll try not to disturb you."

"Good night, Dehlia, Thanks for everything. It was an amazing evening." Elizabeth threaded her arm through Colin's so easily she did not even realize it.

"Night, mom," Colin winked, as he placed his hand over Elizabeth's.

Dehlia blew them a kiss. As she ascended the stairs, they creaked with each step. When Dehlia neared the top of the stairs, she looked down at the pair entering the sun room and smiled broadly.

The moon hung high in the sky. Its pale light illuminated the cozy sun porch enough to create a mystical atmosphere. A half-empty bottle of Harvest Moscato provided a sweet ending to the array of delicious food and hearty country air. Colin and Elizabeth cuddled and drowsed on the rattan settee under the weight of a hand-knit afghan draped over their legs, as the baseboard oil heater succeeded only in taking the edge off the cold.

"Feel like a little walk before we head upstairs? Mom's a little provincial so, while under her roof, her rules." Colin emptied his glass and stood. "I'll keep you warm." His smile melted every objection, and she offered her hand and he pulled her to her feet. She zipped her jacket up to her neck and Colin picked up the blanket before he opened the side door for her and they ventured outside.

Elizabeth felt at home. Throughout the summer, she and Colin and sometimes Dehlia, strolled the paths around the house and gardens after a meal or busy workday. The path from the sun porch led to an idyllic garden that displayed Dehlia's cultivated and most precious flowers. The garden had died down now, but the moon overhead and frosty patches on the walkway had a beauty all their own. When they reached the arbor, Elizabeth saw Dehlia had decorated its entrance with a variety of potted mums in every color of the harvest. "Colin, mums. What a beautiful idea."

"Not as beautiful as you," Colin wrapped the throw around their shoulders cocooning them together and drew her to him and kissed her long with a passion that rivaled that of any in her experience. She returned his kiss and was transported into dreamtime where she remembered the feel of the white mantle on her. Colin broke their embrace and secured the afghan around her. He reached down to pick up a pot of rust-colored mums and handed them to Elizabeth.

"How did you know these were my favorites? Did Marni tell you?" her eyes twinkled.

"Lucky guess. Take them with you for your room." He grinned, his golden brown eyes danced with charm.

The couple followed the path back to the sun porch where once inside, Colin placed the flowers on the table next to the wine and poured a small amount into the bottom of each glass. They returned to the settee and hunkered in. Colin came close to Elizabeth's face which glowed in the extraordinary light.

"Elizabeth, I have loved you since I first saw you drive in through the gates." He handed her the flowers and she looked puzzled.

"You were spying on me?" She was giddy.

"We don't get many visitors." He fidgeted then reached down into the tight cluster of mums and pulled out a box and dropped to his knee.

"Elizabeth Welles, will you marry me?" Colin opened the blue velvet ring box and a massive solitaire caught the moonlight and sparkled brilliantly like the diamonds in the indigo skies.

Elizabeth blinked and did a reality check. "My God, Colin, yes, oh yes." Her eyes were fixed on the perfect stone and she was riddled with small tremors from the shock and the joy. "It's gorgeous. I'm shaking. Is this real?" Elizabeth was babbling and knew with every part of her being that this was right. This was the gift, the blessing, that emerged from years of pain.

He removed the oval-cut diamond from the box. She held out her hand and he slid the ring onto her finger where it would remain until the end of their days together.

Chapter Thirty-Nine

Fruition

Elizabeth admired the lilacs blossoming around the arbor and focused on the pink one she bought for Dehlia all those years ago. It thrived where it was planted, just as she did, and she marveled at how her world had dramatically changed. Elizabeth let her mind retrace the multiple pieces that had to coalesce in order for her life to play out the way it did. She considered the events divine intervention and stood in awe of the amazing force that carved her destiny.

She loved that Colin added the porch swing so she could be nearby and supervise their toddler, Johnathon Douglas, who loved to play in the side yard near the sun porch. She glanced at Marni who shared the swing with her in the dewy spring air. Her face softened into gratitude for their extraordinary bond and life journey. Marni was attentive to her two children playing with Johnathon on a blanket littered with Legos and Hot Wheels. Sophia was four years old and bossy like Marni, making sure Johnathon and Glenn, her younger brother, who were both three, played with the toys the way she thought they should.

Marni sipped iced tea laced with a sprig of mint and turned to her friend. "It's sure muggy today after that squall. You feeling any better?"

Elizabeth was looking forward to the birth of her second child, a girl, in the early fall. "Better than the first few months." She rubbed the mound of her belly that sat high under her rib cage. "Colin's so excited to have a girl. I know she'll be spoiled and Dehlia is already knitting everything pink, as you can imagine."

"Will Doug and Jenna be coming out again when the baby's born?" Marni asked.

"They love it here and are talking about Thanksgiving. We want the cousins to see as much of each other as possible. Dehlia was right about home and family." Elizabeth's mood was wistful.

"I've been preaching that for years and it finally took!" Marni chided her friend.

Glenn threw a plastic car at Johnathon and made him cry. Elizabeth popped off the swing and went to comfort him. "Let's see the boo-boo," and he showed her his arm where there was a faint red mark. She kissed the scratch. "All better."

Marni joined her and squatted down to Glenn's height and told him it wasn't nice to throw things and made him say he was sorry to Johnathon. "Who'd have thought this would be what life looked like even a few years ago?" Marni said, as she picked up toys and put them into a basket. "It's like a dream."

Elizabeth swept up her toddler and took him to the swing and rocked with him in her arms. She lovingly gazed into his honey-brown eyes. "It is, Marni." She squeezed her son and tickled him until wild giggles erupted and he scurried away laughing.

᠅ ᠅ ᠅

The new outbuilding that Colin built for Elizabeth was adjacent to the barn and matched the rustic charm of the older structures in every detail. Elizabeth ordered a carved wooden sign in the shape of an arc that hung over the double door entrance to her studio that read, "Rainbow Studios." When she first moved to Townsend Farms after she and Colin married, she fell in love with the goats and increased the herd after discovering their milk was the basis for elegant skin care products in the forms of soaps and lotions. She found she had the temperament and talent for farm life and an appreciation for the rhythms of nature and embarked upon her own enterprise.

Colin stood in the doorway, baseball cap in hand, watching his wife who was seated at her work bench attaching gold foil labels to bottles of lotion and tying satin ribbons in every color of the rainbow to represent the different scents. Red was a spicy cinnamon, yellow, the fresh lemon verbena, orange, a citrusy tangerine and so on. "Did you and Marni get caught up?" He smiled broadly knowing they texted and talked nearly every day.

"Stop it. It's just fun to watch the kids and have a play day. They change so fast between visits." Elizabeth got up and took a tray full of bottles to a line of shelving near the doorway. "Make yourself useful," she kissed him playfully and shoved the tray toward him. Colin lined up the products according to ribbon color in tidy little rows.

"I came to get you for dinner. Mom said you need to eat." He put on his cap, handed her the empty tray and offered her his arm. She sidled up to him and he caressed her belly. "How's little Priscilla doing?"

Elizabeth rolled her eyes, secured the door and didn't attempt to argue that their daughter would be named Julianna after her mother. They picked their way arm-in-arm toward the main house under a backdrop of sky laden with whipped-cream puffy clouds and a broad rainbow spanning the horizon. Elizabeth imagined the angels working in the splendor of the sparkling rainbow realms watching for those who have despaired and reached out for help and healing. She clutched her husband tighter snuggling her face on his arm and said a silent prayer of thanks.

Acknowledgements

I want to express my gratitude to the helping hands and hearts both seen and unseen who supported and encouraged me to tell this story. Now in the Rainbow realms, I give special appreciation to Rev. Frances Lancaster who always believed in me. And to my editor, Genevieve Olivarez-Conklin, I give praise and gratitude for her meticulous attention to detail and for making me a better writer. And to the cast of colleagues and mentors who have been bright lights along the way, thank you.

About the Author

Marlene King's passion for writing has paralleled multiple professional careers. A sampling of her writing credits include, "Dream Times," a column in *Dream Network Journal* and *The North Kitsap Herald*, and inspirational stories in Simon and Schuster's national bestsellers *Chocolate for a Woman's Soul* anthologies. Other award-winning articles and stories are published in *The Writer Magazine, Intuition Magazine, IASD's Dream Times Journal,* and *Chicken Soup for a Girlfriend's Soul*. Her work was selected for a special edition of *101 Best Stories in Chicken Soup for the Soul*.

She and her husband co-founded a commercial graphics corporation and commercial land acquisition company where she served as corporate executive and administrator. Her art credentials comprise designing promotional print media, logos and graphics, logo design and oil paintings which were exhibited in Northwest Gallery and Illuminarium Gallery and as cover art for *Abundant Living Magazine*.

As an art therapist, Marlene worked in psychiatric and hospice settings, as well as maintained a private practice. She currently facilitates dream groups and is a therapeutic mentor to private clients. She has been a member of the International Association for the Study of Dreams for over 35 years.

Marlene holds a B.A. in Art History, University of California, Santa Barbara and an M.A. in Art Therapy, Marylhurst University.

You may contact her at:

www.dreamtimesguide.com

thedreamplace.wordpress.net